The Shelf Life of a Secret

The Shelf Life of a Secret

Wanda Means

The Shelf Life of a Secret

ONE BLUNT
WOMAN

For information please contact:

www.wandameans.com

Published in the United States of America

Paperback ISBN: 978-0-9998272-0-8

LCCN: 2018903704

1. BIO022000   BIOGRAPHY & AUTOBIOGRAPHY / Women
2. SEL043000   SELF-HELP / Recovery with more specific headings in this section
3. FAM001010   FAMILY & RELATIONSHIPS / Abuse / Child Abuse
4. BIO026000   BIOGRAPHY & AUTOBIOGRAPHY / Personal Memoirs

First Edition

14 13 12 11 10 / 10 9 8 7 6 5 4 3 2 1

Table of Contents

A Few Thoughts, a Few Thanks, and a Few Too Many One-Word Sentences

A few things about me . . .

I'm barely 5'2" and possibly shrinking. In a world of much taller people, this makes my life more challenging. Luckily, almost everyone thinks you're younger when you're short. I have been told I'm muscular—for a girl. WTF? What does that mean, anyway? I'm kissing fifty years old, which means I'm holding on to my forties for dear life. Yes, those are my actual eyes on the cover of this book. Whenever a man tells me my eyes are mesmerizing, I tell him, "Thanks for overlooking the fact that I have small breasts." My thoughts tend to trail off because I have A.D.D. It wasn't actually diagnosed—but, then again, was anyone diagnosed in the '70s with A.D.D.? Don't be surprised when you see one word sentences: it's just my A.D.D. taking over. I'm an extremely loyal person to those whom I love, unless you betray my trust. Trust is not easy for abuse survivors and is not easily given, as it so sacred, but, once you've earned it, the walls come down. It's rare for me to be vulnerable, but I'm human, with a soft side, too. On the flipside, I can be crass and cuss like a sailor. My editor said no more than a hundred F-bombs in the book. I tried, but no promises. You can overlook all the F-bombs in this book, or you can be appalled at my *context*–like my mother ignoring the abuse I suffered–and completely skip over the raw, the real, and the fucking honest *content* in this book. As with anything in this life, we all have a choice. We can choose the path of least resistance, or we can choose the path laden with strategically placed F-bombs. Regardless, thank you for picking up this memoir, or, rather, this self-awareness book. I went to the bookstore, trying to determine which category to put this book in, and I couldn't find the "holy fuck, this one's a mess" section, but I did find the self-actualization/self-awareness section, so let's go with that.

During my seventeen-year marriage, my husband used to always say to me, "You did not just say that!" I'm not sure how many women would start off her book with a quote from her ex, but I've got to give him a lot of credit. He has taken the brunt of many of my verbal blows, so don't be shocked if that exact sentiment crosses your mind a few times in this book. I've never been one to hold back—at least not after the first decade and a half of my life, when I was told to sit still and look pretty. *Wink. Wink.* That was code to keep my mouth shut. My dreaded secret didn't need to be shared. I lived with a vain, narcissistic, selfish woman, also known as my mother. Whenever I spoke to her, she hated my verbal lacerations.

Never mind the facts that I was telling her; the despicable sexual acts her husband had me doing to him. The F-word was simply not acceptable in my home. I still struggle with the content versus context conundrum. When my mother told me at fifteen, "You're ruining this family," I wasn't exactly inclined to say much of anything, for fear of ruining the lives of my family. My mother's words alone were enough to instill the fear of God in me.

I'm quite sure a lot of things came out of my mouth without ever thinking. Technically, it's called lack of impulse control, and it is one of the glorious side effects of childhood sexual abuse. Note: "glorious" is my exemplary sarcasm. Just to be clear, there is NOTHING funny about any child being sexually abused by some sick fuck; however, if I can't find humor in my own personal childhood trauma, I'd go crazy. And I'm crazy enough, as it is. Just ask my boyfriend.

Back to the fascinating human brain—my brain and yours—also known as the last frontier. A brain mixed with a dangerous cocktail of too much fight or flight hormone at a young age interferes with the normal development of a young child's brain. The dopamine involved has the same effects as cocaine, after all. May I introduce you to your amygdala. You'll get to know her in this book. She will enlighten you on your *emotional brain*—a separate area from your wise mind. She controls a major part of you and your decision making.

Take a look back at your own childhood. Ever wonder why you engage in some of the crazy behavior you do? Ever wonder why you can't get out of that mindset once you're in it? If you're dying to know, you can skip on over to chapter six and take the ACE test, to see just how screwed up your childhood may have been. If you're three or below, thank your lucky stars. If you're four or more, let's dig a little deeper. Those numbers reveal a lot about you, your past, your current state of mind, and offers some perspective on how to keep it all in check. No way in hell do I have all the answers, but, *just maybe*, I can give you that aha moment when you realize there's a reason you may be a bit nutty at times.

I've read there are sixty-million of us. *Wait. Sixty-million of whom in the world? Survivors.* That's right, there are sixty-million of us sexual abuse survivors—in America *alone*—walking around right now. Wow! How many of us have ever told anyone? What a shameful secret to keep. I so wish you wouldn't have to harbor that awful secret alone. One of my close girlfriends said to me, "If I could dig up your stepfather's body, I would kill him myself," and I knew, at that moment, I just had to share this story with others. She told me that after I gave her draft number thirty of this memoir. She said the first draft of any book is something one should only share with her therapist. And, sometimes, even *his* therapist. Boys aren't immune to this. Sexual predators don't discriminate sexually. Did you know that pedosexuals (those sick fucks that think sexual relations with children is "normal") want the LGBTQ community to add the "P" at the end of their name? According to them, they have rights, too. Fuck that! Over my dead body.

MANY drafts later and you're reading this one—my self-awareness tell-all (well, not all, but close to it). Writing a book is not only cathartic, but it's a crapshoot. Writing the family Christmas letters was the only practical writing experience I could put on my resume before I started my blog: www.jesusdivorceandoverforty.com, in early 2015. My degree is in finance, not literature. Trust me, I'm no expert at this writing game. I'm barely a novice, but I tend to be a smart ass, and I fully appreciate a well-placed pun. I'm not even creative enough to make up any of these stories. We will leave that up to the JK Rowlings of the world. She is one creative woman! I just recite, relive, and regurgitate most of my life's experiences in a rather filter-less, blunt way. With my fifties knocking on my door, it's fair enough to say I've lived quite a few moments. Some of which are turbulent and some of which are mundane. I'm probably not as fun or crazy as whomever the latest YouTube sensation is, but there is no doubt I've lived nearly fifty years of a roller coaster life.

My story is about yet another woman in her forties, in the middle of a mental *and* emotional breakdown. I'm not going to BS you. Parts of this book are very difficult to read. Parts are very funny. Parts are very tragic. Parts are very heart warming. Parts are eyeopening. Parts are poignant. Parts are devastating. But ALL of it is honest, raw, and real. You may want to get a glass of wine before you dig deep into this book. Or a bottle of tequila. Whatever suits you. Let me be clear about one thing: I am NOT a licensed therapist. I can listen to your stories, and I can help you try to figure out why you're doing the same shit I did, I just can't charge you.

When I first started writing this book, I was two years out of my divorce and in the middle of self-medicating—fucking way too many men (and a couple of women), and still finding myself staring at the bottom of yet another bottle of alcohol. Trust me when I say the ride was fun, even though it was a bit nauseating at times. All of this, and I still had to be a mother to my four children. Yes, all with the same father. I'm crazy, but I'm not that crazy, so don't go there. After all, I started out "normal," but I'm not exactly sure what "normal" means anyway. Suffice it to say that I set out to stay married to the father of my children and raise them together in a loving home. Blah, blah, blah. I'm sure you didn't pick up this book to read about June Cleaver. You want the train wreck, right? I'll give you the train wreck, the dirt, and plenty more.

This book took over two years to write, re-write, and re-write, and, in that time, I was able to evolve. I was able to grow and understand just why I'm so messed up. I was able to understand why I did all the self-destructive things I did to myself, to my children, to my family, and to my friends. I did my damnedest to make the book easy to follow, but I have serious

A.D.D. and tend to get off track sometimes. Thank God for my editor—always reeling me back in focus. I had to start somewhere, so why not start at the bottom of yet another bottle of humility and another dose of pain.

They say most readers don't get past page twenty-eight of a self-help book because their A.D.D. must set in, as well. Luckily, this isn't just a self-help book. It's a self-awareness book with a bit of clinical research to help the reader understand that her childhood issues aren't just "mental, get over it, move the fuck on" issues. Not only are they psychological issues, they are real physiological issues. In order to understand my neurosis, I had to dig deep into my own abyss. Like they say, the higher the wall, the deeper the abyss. I'll introduce you to a twenty-five-year-old study about adverse childhood experiences that should be included in every high school and college curriculum everywhere. "Vice Management 101" should be a required class for every high school freshman out there. We all have vices. Maybe not today, but we will get them. We need to understand how to manage our vices so we don't end up six feet under.

One thing I am certain of throughout this ride: I have a serious issue with pedophiles. They have no business being around our children. They need to be on an island amongst themselves. Have at it there. I don't care. Just stay the fuck away from all children. It's time to change our mindset and start confronting these sick fucks because talking about these uncomfortable topics of the sexual abuse of children should NOT be taboo. I get it, though. The topic is cringe-worthy. Nobody wants to broach this subject. It's uncomfortable. Why are we so uncomfortable talking about it? Isn't that the *real* problem? Why is everyone so afraid to be uncomfortable? Why *can't* we talk about the proverbial elephant in the room, or perhaps the one panting in the sanctuary? There's a lot of information in this book that may make you feel uncomfortable, but it will definitely open your eyes.

If you're an adult who's been abused, I encourage you to keep reading this book. I hope that, by the end, it will give you the courage to talk about it, and you will tell *anyone you trust*. A friend. A lover. A parent. And, eventually, *yes*, your children— once they're old enough to understand. They need to know. What better way to fully understand you? To fully understand who you are? Where you came from and the hell you endured and survived? What do you have to lose? *Nothing*. What do you have to gain? Sanity? Purpose? Freedom? Acknowledgement? Nothing wrong with losing a few extra pounds of guilt! Or is it shame? There is a *big* difference between guilt and shame; I will cover <u>all</u> of this.

TALK TO YOUR KIDS. *Keep* talking. Make it a topic at dinner. Something like this: "Sweetie, Mommy wants you to know it's *NOT* okay if ANYONE touches your private parts. If they do, I'll personally make sure they never use their private parts again. No matter *who* it is. Now eat your peas."

This is not to be ignored, nor swept under the rug. Tell them it is NOT okay for ANYONE to touch them, including *any* person brought into the home, including a parent. And, most importantly, when your kids talk, *believe them.*

I can't get pedophiles to stop their predatory way of being, nor their sexual abuse of children. I wish I could. I'm simply not that powerful. But I *can* start by telling one person at a time to *STOP* being uncomfortable about talking about the sexual abuse of children, because the statistics are staggering: One in three girls and one in five boys will be sexually abused by the time they are eighteen. Let me repeat that: One in three girls. One in five boys.

Next time you're in your daughter's class of twenty-four kids, note that half of those are girls. One third of those (approximately four of them) will be sexually assaulted by the time they're eighteen. Which four will it be? Which one is it happening to *right now?* Can you see it in their eyes? Or perhaps it's *your* daughter. Do you know the signs? What if it's your son? Are you paying attention to the clues? What if it was happening in your own home, and you weren't even aware of it. Can you imagine that for *one moment?* Your child, or one of your friend's children, could have a chance at a reasonably healthy life IF he or she is rescued during the period of abuse. Otherwise, a life of addictions, repeated abuse, and, sadly, sometimes, suicide may be that child's last fateful decision—all because no one believed them, helped them, or rescued them.

Heartbreaking as it is, the odds are fairly high that this is happening to someone you know. It's not just the social media sexual predators, nor the Jared Fogle's and Dr. Nassar's of the world that are abusing our children. Abuse outside the home only account for less than ten percent of all sexual abuse of children. That means the other ninety percent is happening at home. Maybe even someone you love. Would you help if you could? Would you stop it if you knew?

I hope you're uncomfortable imagining all of this. Sometimes we have to feel discomfort in order to shake things up. Let's have an honest and frank conversation.

Would you have stopped it if you knew? Would you have believed me if I told you? What would you have done, once you knew? This isn't just a story about a child who was sexually abused. It's also uplifting, sometimes sad, sometimes funny, and, occasionally, *highly* uncomfortable. I'm here to make all of us think and to make change for the better. To help all those eight-year-olds out there who need to be protected, loved, and validated. Let's start talking about this subject. You. Me. All of us.

I want the taboo to end. If this makes you uncomfortable to talk about this, imagine how the child feels. It's up to us to open those lines of safe communication first. Let's make this less uncomfortable. I want it embedded in these kids' heads that NOBODY TOUCHES THEIR PRIVATE PARTS. EVER!

It's worth it in the end to create this amazing forum of safety to communicate. I can't stress enough, if you're reading this and haven't had a chance to talk with someone, PLEASE open up and talk. You never know, it could be you one day that can truly make a difference in someone's life. It could be a huge awakening for you, as well, and truly set your heart free.

You've heard the saying that, "Good girls don't make history." Well, this nonconforming woman fully plans on making history. I took an unusual path to get here, and I take full ownership of my personal choices that got me here, but I'm here to start this conversation and to make a difference in the lives of those who need it the most.

Chapter 1

Hitting the Bottom of the Bottle, *Again*

"This is not how I am,
I have become comfortably numb"

—"Comfortably Numb," Pink Floyd—

I t's 4 a.m., and I'm wide awake just staring at my bedroom walls. My eyes have adjusted to the darkness, but my heart races in anticipation of my sheer fear of the unknown that darkness can bring. How much longer until the Aleve PM kicks in? I realize it's just another day in my life that ended in downing another bottle of wine and smoking another pack of cigarettes. I can't help but think to myself, "What the fuck am I doing? Where am I *going* with all of this self-sabotaging behavior?" I'm too afraid to even ask where I will end up at this current pace of life.

I'm a divorced woman in the sexual prime of my life. I should be thriving right about now. Yet today, like so many days, I feel as though I don't *thrive* at all—hell, I'm barely surviving. I'm quite sure it wasn't supposed to be this way. I set goals and accomplished them. That is, until my demons took over. I have four amazing kids, and I know I should be a better mother. I should forget the absolute shit-show of a childhood I endured, but sometimes those memories rear their ugly heads, and my conscious mind has led me to yet another deep abyss, and I'm struggling to get out of this one. Again. My mind won't stop, and I know for a fact that all this emotional turmoil is taking control of me and my decision-making. I simply can't take any more of these horrid decisions I continue to make. I have got to get control of my emotional mind, still covered up as my inner child.

This daily analysis comes with the territory. I was sexually molested as a child back in the days when nobody talked about it. It's not like today, when the "#metoo" movement has taken over. Now, we talk about it *ad nauseam*. I can only wonder if we are becoming immune to it. Just turn on the television or open any news app on your smart phone. It's on there, yet, we tend to turn down the volume or simply switch the channel. Every damn day another child is abused, kidnapped, hurt, or killed. I don't even like the word, "molest." In Spanish, "molestar" means "to bother." Believe me, it is WAY more than just bothering some- one. Just once, I wish we didn't sugarcoat the dismal facts. "And in other news, another child was sexually molested." How about, "In other news, a child was forced to get on all fours while her step-father ejaculated all over her." I can see the heads turning now as the reporter shares the grisly details. Yeah right. That's not going to happen anytime soon. Nobody wants to hear the gruesome details, yet children live it every fucking day. Including me. It still haunts me to this day. Maybe not the abuse I endured but just knowing it's happening in so many other homes.

If my life were just about surviving the sexual abuse I endured, I know I could take on that challenge; unfortunately, it's so much more. I am a fighter by nature, but I still feel like I'm constantly being beaten down—so I head for the bottle. Again. And Again. And Again.

So much pain to numb and so little time to do it. I can feel the pain all the way up to the point when I start numbing myself. My soul is continually tested by the roller coaster I'm unable to get off. I find myself asking, "When do I get off this thrill ride?" I rode the merry-go-round for years in my marriage before exiting that ride and getting on the roller coaster. *What was I thinking?* This ride sucks, and it makes me sick. Sure, I thoroughly enjoy the highs, but the lows . . . ? The last thing I needed was another therapist to label me bipolar and start throwing yet another prescription for more white pills to stabilize my moods and dry up my vagina. I know he is just doing his job, but I'm already an addict. I don't need any more addictions. So, why take away my ability to enjoy sex, the one thing that gives me peace, just to make my moods more stable? I'm guessing the good doctor was trying to avoid the lows I experienced that would send my mind to suicidal thoughts. Yes. I said suicide, and that alone frightens me. Why do these thoughts even run through my head? How much longer will these thoughts even cross my mind? I can't take the crying, the drinking, the smoking, and the inevitable suicidal thoughts anymore. These episodes make for really bad days and even worse nights.

Days passed and, again, I sat in the darkness, reeling through another day of unbearable pain. My oldest son came into my bedroom, sat next to me, and just let me put my head on his shoulder. Sobbing. I was unable to talk. He laid there next to me, comforting me. How was this sixteen-year-old boy able to comfort me and listen to me cry, saying, "Mom, it'll be okay?" How can he show me so much love in such a tender moment, but I can't love myself? All I can think about is what a *fucking mess*

I've made of myself. So much hate, so much pain, so little love for myself. I felt so alone in this nightmare. I'm trying to keep my soul in check and *nothing* seems to be working for me.

Another night of hitting rock bottom, but another morning of hope. Hitting rock bottom became one of my many talents. However, getting up time and again also became a valuable skill—one I'd come to treasure much later on. If you choose to come on one of my downward spirals with me, I promise you it won't be fun, especially when the dreaded hangover sets in.

Welcome to the darkness that encompassed my soul for so many years. Something broke in me when my parents couldn't or wouldn't validate, believe, or listen to me when I cried out to them for help. With an absent father, from whom I felt the constant sting of rejection, and a mother who had zero feelings for my pain and insisted I forgive her husband for sexually abusing me, I am perfectly positioned to have more issues than *Vogue.* Of course, Mother thought I should forgive him because, after all, she had. It was the right thing to do, and that's what is expected of us.

REALLY? No. Not for the girl who had a penis shoved down her throat at the age of eight and *God* shoved down her throat for years before that. Forgive an abuser all you want, but she should have kicked his ass to the curb. *That* would've been the right thing to do. As a mother myself, I know how counterintuitive it is *not* to feel called to fiercely protect your children. Children

5

should always feel loved and protected, yet my mother's fear of being alone far superseded everything in her life. Her need for a man in her life trumped her need to be a good mother. Clearly, her need for a man to take her to dinner and make her feel special was a top priority. Nothing beats a great steak on a Friday night when you have a pedophile for a husband. What a tragic message for a mother to send to a child. *"You are not important. Our needs come before yours. Mine and his. Period."*

Decades would pass before I came to realize that I'm a destructive person. Mostly emotionally, and, yes, you guessed it, toward men. Hell, I even tried sex with women, which for me turned out to be a disaster. I learned a new term from my therapist. I suffer from love and sometimes sex addiction, which means I have a propensity to use sex to fulfill me physically and emotionally, even though what I really need and crave is love. Yes, that's a real thing, even if you can't say it without laughing, it's okay. Finally. I can neatly put myself in a box with a label. Surely, now that I know what my actual problem is, I can go fix it. I was up and down like a rollercoaster over the years, fighting with myself internally because I *knew* I was a good person, but I didn't quite *believe* I was a good person.

I learned at a young age that affection and intimacy happen in the bedroom. So, I continued on my never-ending search for a man, a bed partner—anyone to help ease the pain. After all, I was used to pain. I'd become accustomed to it because

I had to. Inevitably, I'd end up choosing the same "type" of men, over and over again, and more painful lessons would ensue. So, I found myself saying *"thank you"* to all the men I'd chosen to assist me in continuing my pain. I was looking for love and faced rejection. After years and years of searching for that "special someone," I thought I might have found him.

Yeah, right. He was not the one. None of them were.

So I moved on, and as each man entered the picture I would think to myself, "This one's 'The One', Wanda. Hang in there! You'll be loved soon." "He" would be full of compliments, and I'd bounce along on a euphoric high. *"I'm madly in love with you,"* he would say in the first few weeks.

But then he would drop the nuclear bomb: "I'm not in love with you after all. I was just experiencing an endorphin rush, you know, an Oxytocin high from all the great sex." Wait, *WHAT? Who says that?*

Finally, one very special man entered my life and rocked my world. I knew without a doubt this man could very possibly be the one I'd been waiting for. He was perfect. Good looking, athletic, intelligent, good father, great in bed, good sense of family—and he made me laugh. *This man gets me,* I would think to myself. *I'm in so deep, I don't know if I could survive this one if it fails.* But with this much passion, comes all the implosions, too. On again, off again, on again, off again. Yet another emotional roller coaster comes to life.

I was drinking more and more to numb the pain and overthinking to quiet the voices in my head. My emotions were all over the place, and I was trying harder than ever to control them, but at this point, I didn't see how I possibly could. I couldn't numb the pain of being rejected all over again. The drinking was out of control, but I couldn't let myself revert to drugs. I had fallen in love and was trapped in this unbearable emotional pain. Pain. Numbness. Pain. Numbness. Surely, as you've been reading this, you've recognized the sad, pathetic, and tragic pattern here.

Due to a series of unfortunate circumstances and some really, *really* bad parenting, I considered ending 100 percent of a life that was only ten percent shit. How could that even be possible? Our minds are so powerful. I knew I would never commit suicide. I adored my children and my life overall; but I knew I needed a release, but I didn't know how to make that happen. I had so much anger over my parents and the abuse I endured, but in all of my attempts at years and years of therapy and talking, it still sat on my soul like an anvil.

At the end of the day, all of it made me numb. We are a product of our parents, and I was sure as hell on my way to being just what they created. If they wouldn't care enough about me to make things right, I had no choice but to figure it out on my own.

Thank God I was able to shut down my brain and fall asleep. Just like clock work, the sun *did* rise again for me. It just happened to be "Suicide Awareness Week." That same week, I saw a post on Facebook—one of the best quotes I have ever read: *"Suicide doesn't take away the pain. It gives it to someone else."* I'm not sure who said that, but I was meant to see it the next morning on Facebook. I ended that night in my emotional mind, but I woke up to my wise mind. Seeing that statement on Facebook shook me to my core.

Luckily, I have a lot of friends, a really good therapist, and several friends who could probably charge me because they take on the role of therapist for me so often. Nobody said life was easy. Oh, sure—we can *make* it look easy. We can paper our Facebook walls and Instagram feeds with all the glossy pictures of the fabulous lives we're leading. We've all heard, "Fake it 'til you make it," but I actually mastered it. We can appear to have everything going for us and still find ourselves staring down the bottom of an empty bottle, or worse, down the barrel of a gun. Fortunately, I don't own a gun and don't have a garage, but anyone can just down a bottle of Tylenol and end it all. How many times have you had thoughts about tempting fate? Simply ending it all.

I have four kids. Yes, four human beings I brought into this world. It's as though happiness skipped over my empty soul and entered *their* little bodies. I would *never* knowingly transfer my pain to them. That's not fair to them and ending my life would merely give my pain to them. So fucking selfish, but the choices I've made over the past few years have only compounded that pain. Ninety percent of my life is good. No, it's great. But that last ten percent—that ten percent is sheer hell. That ten percent is the foundation my parents gave me, the foundation that assured me I wasn't important and my well-being didn't matter.

I had to do something about that ten percent ruining my life. I had to change my mindset and learn to love myself. How the hell does anyone learn to love herself in her mid forties when it hadn't been done the prior four decades? So, I headed to sex and love addiction rehab in Northern California at Five Sisters Ranch. Yes, there is rehab for sex and love addiction. Yes, it's a real issue that needs addressing before it kills you. At the very least, I looked at it as another adventure for this woman in constant need of stimulation. If you're picturing one of those posh spas where they pamper you with one fancy treatment after another, this is isn't one of those places. You're there to work on your pain and stop this never-ending need for sex, love, and validation. During my twelve-day sober retreat, I attempted to dig deep so that I could feel my own value and self-worth. I actually attempted to learn to love myself. As I wrote my entire childhood on ten pages of paper, highlighting the abuse, the abandonment, and the rejection by both of my parents, I reached one epiphany after another. I felt relieved. I felt like I had actually accomplished something. I could actually, finally, love myself.

Then, as the next part of the exercise, we burned the history—all ten pages of it. I found it truly disturbing to discover that it really was possible to fit all the misery ruling and ruining my life on ten pages of paper. Fuck it. Now it was finally over. Time to move on. We even had a ceremony to celebrate my victory over my past and my promised healing. Watching the fire, I could almost feel the ashes actually carry away all of my pain. I would finally love myself, even though my parents couldn't do it. I knew it was up to me, not another person, and certainly not a man.

Well, it worked for about a month. Now what? Back to more drinking? More unfulfilling sex? More numbing my pain? More meaningless relationships with more men? Will I ever be happy? Okay, on occasion, I *am happy*. But I know there's something I need to do and maybe, just maybe, that's what all of this pain and heartache I experienced was for. I decided maybe if I were to start talking and people started to listen, some of my pain would go away. I need to share my painful story, because I know there are people out there who hurt as much as I do. So, I was determined to find a way to release all the pain that dwelled inside me. I wrote down all the many things that hurt me. Then and now.

I wrote down the root of my pain, the list of people I felt I continually let drive my pain, and I buried them under a birch tree I planted in my back yard. Birch trees are known to be trees of renewal, which was very symbolic for me. And now, each day I get to watch that tree grow and bloom with all the pain buried far beneath the surface. I look forward to the leaves falling in autumn, with their array of beautiful colors, and then watching it come back to life in the spring, with my hopes and dreams of better tomorrows. I was really looking forward to the tree maturing and growing, and my hopes with it—but sadly, the tree didn't make it. The roots simply didn't attach. Moving a tree from its nursery then trying to replant it, doesn't always work. Trying to give *myself* new roots, like that birch tree, *also* didn't seem to be working.

A friend of mine told me that birch tree didn't make it because it soaked up all of my sadness. It died for *me,* so I could be rid of all the sadness and pain I'd collected over the years. Be it plants, humans, or emotions, something has to die in order for there to be new growth. And so I said goodbye to all the ill will that has no room in my life, and hello to trees that bloom with hope and love. I have a life worth living without abuse.

As Joan Rivers always said, *"Can We Talk?"* I'm going to talk about taboo things very few people are willing to talk about. Secrets should absolutely have a shelf life. Take the preservatives out of your secrets so they don't live forever inside of you, as they do maim you—or worse. Yes, they can even kill you.

I'm speaking from a much better place today than where I was before. Some say it's because I may have opened up too much, and I would most definitely have to agree. Just to be clear, this is NOT a self-help book. This is a memoir about my lost childhood—more like my interrupted childhood—with special sections to share what I learned on my journey. I still managed to escape some of my "chores" at home and have fun. I was just forced to do so, harboring a very dark secret. A secret I kept for far too long, and as you'll find out, finally sharing my secret bit me in the ass. The sting of that bite has scarred me to this day.

I still have issues. I don't know if they'll all ever really go away. I believe God tests us at every turn. It would be naive of me to think everything will be jolly for the rest of my life. I wish I could say those thoughts will never creep into my head again, but they could and most likely will. I fully expect life to rear its ugly head. It may be my doing, and that's one thing I am fully cognizant of today. We are here to learn from our experiences, and I for one am going to make *sure* I don't hit rock bottom again. But either way, I won't be defined by those moments. I'm constantly reinventing myself, for both my children and for my sanity. They *deserve* a balanced mother who's there for them. And I deserve to be a balanced woman.

Personally, I choose not to be a weak woman. Just because I came from extremely weak people, it doesn't mean I am required to be weak. I like being strong and testing my limits. I want you to ask yourself, what are *your* limits? I think you would be surprised if you pushed them ever so slightly—whatever that looks like in your world. We all reach rock bottom at one time or another in life. Just don't reach the bottom of a bottle of alcohol or pills. Don't let that be your bottom. Don't reach a point where your mind wants to end it all. Life is worth living, and there is some-one out there who can help make a difference. There is *always* someone out there who can come to your rescue. Don't give up.

Don't indulge yourself to a point in your life that you become numb to facing your problems. They never go away.

You have something to say, so say it. You have something to do, so do it. But do *NOT* give up. I didn't. I would never transfer my pain to my children. It's my job to shield and protect them and certainly NOT allow the pattern of abuse in my family to be repeated.

That ten percent is the foundation my parents gave me, the foundation that assured me I wasn't important and my well-being didn't matter. I was almost willing to take away 100 percent of a good life that was only ten percent off balance. That foundation has seeped its poison into every aspect of my relationships. The years of highs and lows in my relationships have taken their toll on my soul. Trying to find "the one" has led me to the extreme lows that framed much of my 40s. I want off this ride. I want peace and understanding.

How did I get here? I already know the answer to that question but now what? Did my traumatic childhood really have that much impact on me? My emotions are all over the place. I'm trying harder than ever to control them, but, at this point, I don't see how I possibly can. I've come to another fork in the road of my life. Where am I going to go from here?

Part 1

ACEing Abandonment, Abuse, and Neglect

•

My Childhood

Chapter 2

Daddy,
Where Did You Go?

"You left me just when I needed you most"

—"Just When I Needed You Most," Randy VanWarmer—

"Daddy's home!"

These are happy words in an average home—but words I never heard. Forty-eight years later, I'm writing a 60,000+ word book because I never heard those two words. I suppose that seems to be a fair trade. Dad left. Big deal, fathers leave all the time. I now have my own four kids I have to raise and tell myself to just focus on them. "Move on, Wanda," I hear my own voice say over and over. I so desperately wish it were only a matter of moving on.

Once Daddy left, I thought surely my mother would step in, to carry the load and shield me from the pain of our broken family and fill that tremendous void where love was abandoned. I fully expected to be rescued from major childhood trauma number one. If only. . . .

It was early 1970 in Dallas, Texas, and the door to our home had swung wide open. Out walked my father, who happened to be husband number one for my mother, but several more husbands would follow. Just like that, Daddy was gone. Apparently, for my father, there was no end in sight to the overwhelming responsibilities that accompanied the four children he had just fathered: his six-year-old son, four-year-old son, one-year-old daughter, and me, a three-month-old baby. The pressure of raising four tiny children could send any mere mortal walking; freedom from this pressure seems so liberating.

But my father didn't leave to be free of the burdens of raising children. He left his own family—the family he co-created—for another family. He walked right out of one door and into another, literally. Behind the second door, was just another woman and another set of problems. The "other woman" had her own three children who already had a father. Now her children had two fathers. That's two fathers for them and zero for my siblings and me. This is how the imbalance of my life began. Let this also be known as childhood trauma number one.

According to my mother, I was an accident. My only reason for being here was because she failed to use her birth control. Somehow, she failed to understand that birth control does not work by osmosis. You don't just set your birth control on the bedside table next to you and expect it to be effective. Sadly, all my mother's "unwanted" pregnancy did, was prolong my father's exit strategy by nine months. Nine months can be an eternity with the wrong person, but we all know a "good man" would never leave his pregnant wife. Leaving your wife while she's pregnant isn't a good look, no matter what anyone says . . . and we all know looks are important in the South, where I'm from. Public appearance became a bitter life lesson that continually haunted me for years to come. This is where my father's ounce of decency came in: the other woman, my soon-to-be stepmother, and her children waited for a more appropriate time for my father to leave us. They all had to keep up appearances. As you can imagine, this caused a lot of mental anguish for my mother, carrying an unborn child, knowing full well of his indiscretion.

Some neurologists believe that trauma, to an expectant mother, can adversely affect a child in utero. As the human brain develops, so does the *amygdala*. The amygdala is an almond-shaped set of neurons located deep in the brain's medial temporal lobe and plays a key role in processing emotions. Part of the limbic system in the brain, the amygdala is the very place we store love, hate, and fear. It's inconceivable that all of those emotions are stored in a tiny place in our brains the size of an almond. If the almond is traumatized or over-stimulated during fetal development, it can grow at an abnormal rate and forever affect the emotional decisions of that person. As I like to say, these decisions are really reactions, or, more often, overreactions. We are better off using our frontal cortex for the really important life decisions—you know, those *really* big ones, like the person you choose to spend your life with.

However, when the amygdala takes over, look out! Some seriously shit decisions are bound to happen. Have you ever sent a drunk text to an old lover and wholeheartedly regretted it the next day? That was your amygdala. Let's call my amygdala "Amy the Almond" going forward. Amy has ruled my decisions more than I care to admit, but Amy is truly one *stubborn* bitch. If your inner-Amy is an abnormal size, try not to be so hard on yourself. I highly recommend you watch an absolutely awe-inspiring TED talk by Robert Sapolsky, "The Biology of Our Best and Worst Selves."[1] He discusses the amygdala, epigenetics, the frontal cortex and the biological development of the brain and how it affects our everyday decision-making. I can't stress how important this is to your overall understanding of you, your brain, and your behavior. Robert Sapolsky states, "Every bit of behavior has multiple levels of causalities." I suggest you take the time to watch. He goes on to say that if your mother has stress during utero, the epigenetics that turn on some genes while turning others off will develop your amygdala to be more excitable as an adult and elevate your stress hormone levels. I suppose knowing her husband was sleeping with his secretary, caused her stress hormones to elevate. Not a good start for my amygdala. It's already off track and I wasn't even born yet.

As I grew older, there was very little care given to my emotional growth. I have very few childhood memories of my father, as I only saw him a few times a year. My father had another family who needed him, after all, and my mother was busy playing musical chairs with husbands. I was shuffled around from one "home" to another with my mother. I always wondered why I had to live with my mother and her revolving door of men. At my young age, I didn't realize that home could be a moving target. Why wasn't my home with my father? I couldn't grasp why it was impossible for us to all share. So, I often uttered the

1. https://www.ted.com/talks/robert_sapolsky_the_biology_of_our_best_and_worst_selves

words, "When are you coming home, Daddy?" Daddy is a very Southern way to address a father, especially in Texas. No matter where he lived, he was always Daddy to me. I wanted him to love me—to *really* love me. Deep down, every little girl just wants to know her daddy loves her. A little unconditional love goes a long way. Sadly, I had no idea what unconditional love felt like. I knew what *conditional* love felt like, but I also knew it wasn't the same.

With the ink was still drying on my parents' divorce papers, my father married the other woman—who was also his secretary—in December of 1970. It seems idiotic, in retrospect, that something so tragic for me is so cliché. As part of the divorce, my parents made a life-altering deal that is simply incomprehensible to me today, as a mother: my mother took the girls and my father the boys. Even then, I couldn't fathom how anyone could make that deal. I understand that four children is a lot at once—I have four of my own. The fact that my siblings and I were forever separated for my stepmother's convenience, though, is beyond my realm of understanding. *Her* children weren't separated. My father and his former secretary kept *her* family intact. The fact that we were separated was so mind-boggling and so unfair to me, even at that young of an age.

My sister and I did spend a couple of weeks in the summer with their newly formed family, and all four of us would finally be together for just a few days a year. For all those years and all those summer visits, I was desperate for my father to want me. It just wasn't in the cards. When I was with my father's new family, I was baffled by the fact that his new wife—his former secretary—had such significant power over him, considering that she had been "the help" at one point. Don't people who are overly concerned with appearances know you don't fraternize with the help? She made it clear, to my father and to us, that she didn't want us around. She hardly acted like a mother to my brothers, much less to me, and they lived with her. Healthy women don't feel threatened by a child, but I was constantly made to feel like I was second to her and her children. While her kids got cars, braces, college educations, and basic love, my brothers got kicked out of the house.

When I was six years old, my father told me it was imperative that I accept Jesus Christ into my heart as my Lord and Savior. I was more than happy to oblige; I thought this was finally a way to get close to him. By doing as he asked, I was conveying, "I love you, and now *you* can accept me." Many a Christmas would come and go, and I'd get a few minutes of his time. I always felt as though I had to compete for his love and attention. No child should ever have to fight that battle, and I still think, to this day, "What the hell was *wrong* with you, Daddy?" When my sister and I lived in Plano, Texas, we were only five miles from my father's home. Five measly, short—walkable if you had to—miles. Despite the close proximity, my father came to *maybe* one or two of my volleyball and soccer games. It won't surprise you that he attended almost all of his step-children's games. I felt slighted again and again and again. I was always looking in the stands for him, and always disappointed to see he was never there. There was always that painful sting of rejection, that fear of never being good enough. Of being unworthy. Even today, I still feel the emotional pain of his rejection. Damn, my Amy is such a dysfunctional almond.

I vividly remember, years later, when one of my stepbrothers got married. The four of us (my real brothers and sister) were actually altogether, which was unusual. We were rarely all in one place at the same time, since my mother constantly moved my sister and I from one man's home to another. My dad, my brothers, my sister, and I took a brief moment to escape the madness of the wedding festivities and decided to take a few snapshots together. It was just the five of us. A man and the four children he fathered. This was the mid '80s and well before smart phones, so there were no selfies, no quick view of the shot, and certainly no instant gratification. This was so old school, we needed a 35mm camera loaded with film. You remember those—in order to see the photos you had to take them to be developed. Imagine the thought of actually having to wait for your photos to develop so you could see them? I was so excited to get that one memory of all of us together—the family that should have been.

Alas, I never did see any of those pictures. They mysteriously disappeared. Why was something that should have been so simple and easy to obtain taken away once again? It was just a *photo*. I wanted a memento of *our* family for my siblings and me. Wanting the littlest things in life shouldn't be so incredibly complicated. Yet, my want for something so simple led my family to claim I was difficult. It's a shame. I was obviously asking too much to have a picture taken of my daddy and me. I had craved a simple moment like that one, and when I finally got it, it was taken from me. And, no, I don't even have a picture of just me with my mother and father. Not one. It makes sense when you consider that throughout my entire life I've never even seen them say two words to each other.

I still have so many unanswered questions for my father. He only "showed up" for fifteen minutes a year, and that gave me hope that he actually loved me. That left 525,575 minutes each year that I felt hopelessly rejected by the one man who was supposed to love me unconditionally. Now, I'm forever wondering why I wasn't good enough, why he left forty-eight years ago to raise another family, leaving the one he created behind. My father was my only hope of having a connection with any of my male parents. I would have hoped that perhaps I could have connected with just one of my mother's five husbands.

Pedophilia doesn't count as a connection.

I'm constantly reminded how incapable—or unwilling—my father was of showing me any type of love. I'm now five for five in the never-experiencing-what-a-true-father's-love-feels-like department. I know many others out there resonate with these very deep feelings of loss and rejection. I wish I knew what to do with all this rejection. These emotions are like floodgates, slamming open and shut again. It hurts, and I know holding on to this anger only hurts *me*. Sometimes I wonder if it's anger—or simply sadness. Is it the anger of my father never being there or the sadness of not getting the love I so desperately deserved?

I'm offering you a full view of all the craziness, the dysfunction, and the very questionable—often salacious—details of my life. It all started with an innocent little girl reaching out for her daddy. My first childhood trauma—my father's constant rejection of me year after year—was the foundation of my youth, and adversely affected me for years to come. The very foundation of my youth had more than just cracks in it—it was poorly built and full of gaping holes. With a history like mine, it's easy to take daddy issues to a whole new level. Trust me, as a homebuilder with over twenty years of experience, I do know what that is all about. If you screw up the foundation of a house, it is quite likely that you are going to have problems with the *entire* house. And, yes, this also applies to human beings—a truly fitting metaphor here. It's one thing to be sexually abused by one man and ignored by my mother, but constant rejection by my own *father* was simply too much to bear.

Chapter 3

Snow Days Blow

**"There's been a load of compromisin'
on the road to my horizon . . ."**

—"Rhinestone Cowboy," Glen Campbell—

After my mother's third failed marriage, unlucky number four—Jim—entered the picture. Suddenly, there were no more musical chairs with the men. No more revolving doors. This husband would stick around for the next thirty-five years. Enter childhood trauma number two.

In 1978, we lived in Madisonville, Kentucky. I had never been to nor had I ever heard of Madisonville, Kentucky. It had a population of fewer than 20,000 people. There were a few good churches, and church was very important. Church was required. Our family lived on the edge of town, and behind us were miles and miles of fields. To an eight-year-old, they seemed to go on forever. We really did live in a pretty place. Small. Quaint. Small-town America, where everything was good, and evil lived elsewhere. Nobody ever broke into our home, and we were safe from outsiders. Why would anyone think you needed to be protected *inside* the home? As a child, I was certainly afraid of ghosts and monsters under my bed, but who knew the real monster was an adult man in the bedroom next to mine? Our parents are supposed to protect us from the *real* monsters, but that didn't happen in my case.

It was just a small town in the middle of the nowhere with very little to do—unless you're a kid who loves snow in the winter. There was lots of winter snow, and when the snow came, it stuck around for a while. There was very little equipment to plow the roads in small town Kentucky, so snow days were plentiful. Kids love snow days. In the late '70s, video games were nowhere near conception, so kids still played outside. All day, sun-up to sun-down. When I was a kid, with weeks of snow and no school, that meant weeks of good old-fashioned outdoor play. I had a red sled, which I loved, and was always out playing in the snow. As an eight-year-old child, I couldn't fully understand why mother always had to work on those snow days. Now, it's clear as mud that dietitians didn't get snow days. The patients in the hospital where she worked still had to eat, so they still needed her there. So off to work she went. Rain, snow, or shine. My stepfather was another story. He was an engineer and also in the construction business. Work ceased on snow days. Few things strike fear in the heart of an abused child like knowing her stepfather's intentions on days his wife is gone to work all day and the kids have had to stay home from school.

For most kids in America, a snow day meant a day off. A free day. A fun day. Not for me, though—I had to perform. What a terrible way to describe the life of an eight-year-old. I did my best to stay outside and play, but when I went inside, there were things required of me. Things I didn't want to do, nor does any kid. Many days of my childhood began in the same, terrible way. It was cold outside, but I didn't care. I was already numb. Even in freezing temperatures, anything the outdoors had to offer was certainly better than anything indoors. Even today, this holds true for me.

Being woken up before 6 a.m. at the age of eight with a tongue between my legs is something I will never forget. I've tried to remember the first time it happened, but I can't. I wish I could. That way, I could remember how this entire shit storm started. You know, like the first time you puked when you got drunk. Or an anniversary, perhaps, like when someone dies and we call it the "anniversary" of their death. This was mine.

This marked the end of my childhood innocence. I was a sweet, young, third-grader who had only eight years of childhood innocence. As he had his way with my little body, he would pick me up and take me to the couch in the living room. I never understood why he pulled me out of my bed— my safe place. My own bed, where I thought it was safe until he came in my room. That was *my* room, and he had *not* been invited. My bedroom was the one place I could call my very own. The selfish fuck had destroyed that, too. I will never be able to think of my bedroom as a safe place—no matter what bedroom, no matter what house, no matter what age. I never understood how he could have taken that from me. It had always been my safe haven until the first morning he intruded. I'd been so certain my blanket protected me from the evil monsters.

Jim would take me to the living room and put me on the couch. He'd position me on all fours like a dog, with my behind high in the air, and then ejaculate on me. He would place his right knee on the couch and his left leg would stand on the floor. The monster's milky semen would squirt all over me. I would just lay there in utter silence. When he was finished, I was allowed to run to the bathroom to clean up the mess. An eight-year-old girl left to clean up a fifty-year-old man's literal and metaphorical mess. I can never forget the smell because it never leaves you. The smell of the milky white substance I had to wipe off of my bottom and the residue that drifted down my legs. I suppose that was gravity just doing its job. One tissue would never do the work; it was a two-tissue job, always. I would flush it down the toilet and think to myself, *"There, all gone,"* like it never existed. I never even stopped to think about this ritual. I just learned to be grateful it was over for another day, having no idea what tomorrow would bring. When my mother and sister woke up in the mornings, I didn't dare say a word. The shame consumed me. The silence grew inside me like a cancer. My mother and sister slept footsteps away from the horror that I was experiencing right outside their bedroom doors, yet they were completely clueless. They were completely in the dark. Just like me. I would eat breakfast as quickly as I could, and then I would head outside. Outside was the only place where I felt safe. I was safer in the street, whether it was snowing or not. I *always* felt safer outside.

One of my saddest memories of a snow day was the day I wanted a backpack. It was a *cool* backpack. It had the school logo and mascot on it—we were the Broadway Elementary School Bobcats. I never had anything this cool, and I *had* to have it. Today, every kid has a mass collection of T-shirts from everything they do and every event they attend. Back then, it was rare to have anything with your school logo on it. I distinctly remember pulling the signature form out of my folder. My mom had already left for work, but not my stepfather. Another snow day meant another closed-down construction site and another day he didn't have to go to work. As I handed him the form, all I could think about was how excited I was—he signed it, and I was going to get my backpack! I'm sure I was panting like a puppy about to get a treat. He took the form and read it. I remember saying to him, "I really want it."

Jim looked down at me with his disgusting, fat stomach and what little was left of the wiry grey hair that made up his famous comb over and said, "If you lick me." *If you lick me.* I may forget a lot of things in this lifetime, but I'll never forget that. His words are still vivid and everlasting. I wish I could forget this moment, but I can't. What bravado this man had. One would think he might be concerned about the fact that my sister could have walked in at any moment. But he knew he was safe; she was already outside, and it was just the two of us in the house.

That was my very first blowjob. I was eight-years-old. And, trust me, it was a job. Done. Job complete. I remember thinking to myself, *"How many more times am I gonna have to do this? Will I have to do this every single time I want or need something? Should I go ahead and put this on my resume? Oh wait, I'm only eight, I don't need a resume yet."*

But I did get the new backpack I so desperately wanted. I worked for it. I earned it. It was mine. Lesson learned. Unfortunately, the lesson I learned is if you want something badly enough, there is a costly price to pay for it. That lesson would resonate with me for years to come.

Chapter 4

The Elephant Panting in the Sanctuary

"Take me to church. . . . I'll worship like a dog at the shrine of your lies"

—"Take Me to Church," Hozier—

The dreaded whistle. You know the one: the two-fingers-in-your-mouth whistle with a pitch so high the dogs run away. It's unmistakable and was always my call to go inside. I hated having to go inside. I felt free outside. I felt unencumbered and able to play. Outside, there was no one to bother me, touch me, or force me to do unthinkable things. In retrospect, the irony of it all is that outside, balls were my friends. The volleyball, basketball, football, or baseball. Just about any ball would do to keep me busy and away from *his* balls. When the whistle blew, though, I *had* to go inside for dinner. And dinner meant sitting across the table from him.

Imagine having dinner every single night, your mother perched in his lap, draping her arms around him. My mother was so pretty, and it took her an hour and a half each day to get dressed (that didn't include washing her hair, but then it took a lot of time and effort to get that football-helmet hairdo that Sally Field wore in *Steel Magnolias*). The woman never set foot in a gym, but she wasn't overweight at all. She lacked any sort of muscle tone and any sort of athletic prowess. The first time she played softball, she tripped over first base. Nonetheless, I always thought my mother was very pretty. I never understood how an unattractive, balding man with a huge gut and serious man boobs was ever able to get a woman like her. I'm sure the Benjamins had something to do with it, since Jim had more money than she ever made. I don't mean to sound shallow. Looks aren't everything, but this guy used to mow the lawn in his *blue speedo* (aka banana hammock). That, alone, should have been cause for a divorce. Or, the fact that I was thirteen then and had already told my mother that he had been molesting me for two years.

Jim was husband number four, and, to lucky me, he was just another man across the table to sit and stare. Except this one wore no shirt, had a large white belly, and a comb-over. The little hair he had left was thinning and greying. *Quite the looker,* as you can imagine. He had an awful, abrasive, Yankee accent. My mother would kiss him all over. I just sat there, staring, knowing he was waiting to be alone with eight-year-old me. I saw no end in sight and no reprieve coming my way anywhere in the near future, but I didn't dare say a word. I would just sit there numb and motionless, watching their disgusting tongues play with each other. *Gross.*

I can still hear the ice rattling and the clinking glasses as they would toast their newfound love—a clear liquid in his glass, a brownish liquid in hers. He drank vodka and she drank scotch. It would take everything in me not to let my eyes roll back in my head, as they'd surely get stuck there, and I'd look like a monster. Every kid has nightmares of evil, one-eyed monsters invading their room. Luckily, most kids wake up from their nightmares untouched, assured their nightmare was just a figment of their imagination. Unfortunately, that wasn't the case for me. My monster was very real and came to visit often.

As I would sit there at the table, I would cope by letting my thoughts wander. The child in me said, "Really? I'm eating. Do you have to do this now? At the dinner table?" My thoughts were the simple ones of a child with so much hope and so much life ahead of her. My world was very isolated back then. There was no instantaneous anything; instead, there was a lot of down time. There was no internet, no social media, no Insta-whatever, and, consequently, no immediate gratification. And, sadly, no one to talk with about something so awful. *Shhh . . . can you keep a secret?* I mean a *really big* secret? There were simply things we didn't talk about back then. *Nobody* talked about them. This kind of pain grows like a weed inside of you, and there is no one to share the horror with—this awful, dark secret.

We always dutifully headed off to church to free ourselves of the guilt and shame, but not the pain. Never the pain. The pain lingers. The preacher would assure us, "Your sins are forgiven! Now go home, free of sin." *Oh, please.* I would sit there, not listening, aware even at my young age of how duplicitous their lives were. Adults made a *"wah wah wah wah"* noise in Charlie Brown television cartoons, and this was only amplified for me because of what I knew. I listened and thought about what an awful sinner this man *really was*. Kids don't listen to adults very often, so why bother with words when you know this whole exercise is just for appearances?

I reached a point where I couldn't take the rambling of the preacher at all. My childhood was filled with a lot of Jesus.

Lots of sin, lots of evil, and a lot of bad choices, but Jesus couldn't stop the evil. Apparently, Jesus was only able to forgive evil, not prevent it. Since my earliest childhood memories, Jesus had been shoved down my throat, figuratively, and all the while a penis was shoved down my throat, *literally*. All of these mixed messages came from a disgusting slob who was sick in the head.

Sunday meant that football immediately followed church. When the Cowboys played at noon, the minister did his damnedest to cut the sermon short so we could all make it home in time for kickoff. It always struck me as odd that he had no issue sharing with the congregation that that's what he was doing. The only time we ever skipped brunch on Sundays was when it was a noon game day, but a three-o'clock game meant there was still time for brunch. I was always in a dress those days, with my short hair curled. I was every bit a tomboy, and tomboys don't like to wear dresses. They *certainly* don't like hot rollers in their hair with those damned u-shaped pin holders—the ones that pricked your scalp when your mother shoved them into your head, to get your hair perfect. All I could think about was that no one offered me a suitable answer as to why I *couldn't* wear my Adidas shoes and red shorts to church, sporting my favorite T-shirt featuring me and JR Ewing. My mother made me wear taffeta to church. I hated taffeta because cheap taffeta is scratchy. My mother wanted perfection. She wanted a perfect, happy family unit, and by the looks of things, she had it. Jesus was perfect, so we had to *be* perfect and we had to *look* perfect for church. No apparent flaws allowed. This taught me that you were allowed to be flawed, but you weren't allowed to show your flaws. I was expected to sit up, shut up, bow my head, and pray. They wanted me to pray for forgiveness, but I didn't understand what I needed to be forgiven for.

When church was over, and we headed to the car, I noticed a shift the second the car doors closed. We were still in our parking space when my stepfather loosened his tie. I've often wondered why men start their day with a noose tied around their necks. With each yank of his tie, I would see his large, white, fleshy belly in my mind. He began to relax once church was over and I began to get anxious. Let the games (or *sins*) begin. There would always be next Sunday for forgiveness. People could do whatever they wanted because there was always next week for absolution, even if the other 99.5% of the week was full of sin. I'm assuming most mathematicians do not go to church, or else someone would surely have pointed out how badly the scales are tipped. Jesus, the "perfect one." Where was Jesus when I needed him? My youth was my hypocritical upbringing. My mother made damn sure we went to church every Sunday, rain or shine. She didn't seem to grasp the fact that church was just a building—one filled with sinners and with more people who couldn't protect or help me. I couldn't have been more confused. This was so much more than just the metaphorical elephant standing in the room. *My* elephant was panting in the sanctuary, disguised as a fifty-year-old pervert.

Where was my mom? Why couldn't she see this? She was married to this monster. How was I going to tell her?

Chapter 5

Telling an Emotionally-Impotent Mother My Secret

"I can hear her now sayin' she ain't gonna have it. Don't matter how you feel, it only matters how you look."

—"Mama's Broken Heart," Miranda Lambert—

In 1983, I was twelve years old. *Something about Amelia,* starring Ted Danson, was on TV and I was alone in my room, wondering if now was the time to tell my mom. The abuse had stopped when we moved from Kentucky back to Dallas. My mother and I had moved around a lot: from husband to husband, apartment to apartment, home to home, and city to city. There were four elementary schools, four husbands, and four children. I wasn't even a teenager, and we had moved so many times that I can't clearly remember it all now.

I can remember that back in my somber, vanilla Dallas bedroom, I had a thirteen-inch black and white television. It had an antenna that stretched to about three feet and had one rod pointing up and one pointing forty-five degrees in the other direction, but it worked. My television was the only entertainment I had in my room. The walls were bare because my mother wouldn't let me tape any pictures or posters on them. Every other little girl my age had a poster of Rob Lowe from *St. Elmo's Fire* in her bedroom. I wanted one, too.

My bedroom was furnished with old furniture from my mother's aunt. The furniture was brown (still to this day I *hate* the color brown). The headboard of my bed rested against the wall connected to my mother and the pedophile's bedroom. Throughout my childhood, I felt the need to move my bedroom furniture around about every three months. I was sure if I moved my bed around, it might confuse him, and he wouldn't know where to find me. Ah, the optimistic thinking of a child. To this day, I still move my furniture around often, including in my daughters' rooms. No one will *ever* touch them. Ever.

Something About Amelia is about incest. In the movie, Ted Danson's character molests his daughter. For the record, I hate the word *incest*. It makes me think of two siblings in the backwoods of nowhere, engaging in consensual sex. I'm acutely aware the standard remainder of this joke is "in the backwoods of Kentucky," but I'm not amused, for obvious reasons. *Gross.* Clearly, I'm indignant about the word. I was molested. His contact with me *wasn't* consensual. I was sexually abused. As a child. By an adult. But the movie motivated me, so I thought, *"Now's the time. I'm going to do it. I'm going to tell her."*

Let me give you a visual of me at that time: I was still a very little girl. Even though Wanda was my given name, everyone called me Beth. My mother hated the name, "Wanda," but that was the deal she made with my father: if my sister was to be named after my mother's mother, then I was to be named after my father's mother. I barely weighed sixty pounds. I had no boobs, hips, or hair anywhere. Nothing whatsoever that would indicate I was anywhere *near* being a woman. The pediatrician had said that on a scale from one to five for physical maturity, I was a two. There were no tampons for me in middle school; I was still *three years* from puberty. I sat there in awe, watching this movie. I couldn't believe this was on TV. I couldn't believe this really happens to other girls, too. It was time to tell my mother the secret I had been keeping for the last two years. I knew, without a doubt, deep in my heart, she would protect me. She would tell him to stay the hell away from her daughter. I was going to be saved from this horrible man. Finally, I had hope.

When the movie was over, I turned off my television and tried to wipe the tears off my face. I reached for a tissue and realized this was more than a two-tissue job. I had no idea at the time this would be *way* more than a two-tissue job; it would last for the rest of my life. I should've bought stock in Johnson & Johnson. The physical mess could always be cleaned up with a couple of tissues, but the emotional mess caused that day never went away.

With an inspired courage and confidence, I was no longer reluctant to open my bedroom door and make that six-foot trek across the hall to their bedroom. I saw their door was open and walked right in, like I had many other nights, to say good night to my mother. I asked her to come to my room because I needed to tell her something. I knew I was about to turn her world upside down, but I needed her to believe me, to take care of me, and, more importantly, to rescue me. This time was different. Instead of me telling my mother goodnight, she came to my bedroom and sat down beside me on my bed. The tears were streaming down my face as I tried, crying uncontrollably, to get the words out. I said, "Mom, I need to talk to you. I was watching this movie where the dad . . . um . . .

touches his daughter in her private area." As I paused, I got no response from her. All I could see was a blank stare on her face. This wasn't easy for me because I had never uttered a word to anyone about what had been happening to me. Based on her reaction, I knew I needed to just come right out and tell her. So I told her. "Mom, Dad touched me in my private area. He did things to me when we lived in Kentucky." I had finally said it.

The blank stare on her face turned to complete shock. As I was trying to get more words out in between the sobs, she interrupted me and said, "I don't understand," and then she got up from my bed and walked out. Then, the molester came into my room, but, this time, with different intentions. He looked me straight in the eye and *ordered* me to go into their bedroom and tell her none of what I had just told her was true. He demanded that I *recant*. And I did. I marched into their bedroom with tears dried on my cheeks, and told her none of it was true. And that was that.

I was inches from having a real relationship with my mother—a deep, sincere, emotional, and meaningful relationship. If you wonder why I would go back and recant my story, remember, *I was thirteen years old*. I felt like I didn't have a choice. I had tried to reach out to my mother and that shit blew up in my face. So, we went about our lives. Luckily, he was traveling five days a week and the abuse *had* stopped two years prior. But I was on to him, and he knew it. I wouldn't let him near me. It didn't stop him from grabbing my sister's ass in front of my mother. To this day,

I'm dumbfounded that it never struck a chord with her. I didn't have a "safe zone" to say anything. I had been shut down by *both* of them, and I couldn't verbalize the disgust I was feeling.

I don't remember what my mother was like before my step-father came into the picture. I do vividly remember being a young girl and needing my mother's love and attention. I also remember what an angry person she became over the years. I watched it get worse every single day. I have often wondered if it was because she stayed with him. Perhaps it was her only way to vent; I don't know. Maybe she was so angry because she was still so deeply in love with my father, but he had stranded her with four children. She never said what caused her to be so angry, and, with time, it became worse.

Three years later, in the spring of my freshman year of high school, we were living in Arizona. I *hated* Arizona because I hated leaving all of my friends in Dallas. I would have done anything to move back to Texas, so I decided to tell her about the abuse *again*. This time, there were no tears. I wanted to leave Arizona. I wanted my mother to leave this pedophile, and, more than anything, I wanted to stop feeling so disgusted that she chose to stay with this sickening man.

"Mom, remember when I told you about that movie I watched and what happened to me when we lived in Kentucky? And remember when he came in and went back out, and I told you it didn't happen? Well, it *did* happen. He did a lot of bad things to me."

I'll be damned if this time she didn't actually *believe* me. Victory! I envisioned my sister, my mother, and me moving back to Texas, with the pedophile long gone! *Hasta la vista!* But . . . it didn't quite pan out that way. Instead of packing our bags and fleeing from this evil man, my mother turned to me and said, *"You are ruining this family, and you should be ashamed."*

Are you fucking kidding me? Now she knew the truth, she still didn't validate me, and I was stuck in Arizona. There went my plan to get the hell away from him and back to Texas. I *needed* for her to extricate this man from our lives. I was no longer inches from any sort of meaningful relationship with my mother—I was *miles* away, and felt in every way like a betrayed daughter. It was hard enough to gather the courage and confront the situation, but, true to form, she made *me* feel ashamed, instead of shaming him for what he had done to me. It's what any mother, even a below-average one, would do when her daughter tells her that *her* husband put his dick in her mouth!

Of course, I didn't state it quite like that, but it *is* what he did. No more Ted Danson movies for me. Except for *Cheers*—that made me laugh. Well, *Cheers to you,* Wanda, no one believes you, and, when they do, no one does anything about it. I couldn't believe some of the things she had the audacity to say to me after that. "He paid for your college tuition. Isn't that enough? You need to forgive and move on." My favorite quote from her was, "This, too, shall pass." If she'd only been able to hear how I'd finish that sentence in my head: "And so might I." I still use the quote, "This, too, shall pass," today. In reality, it is a logical statement, but my sadness and my anger have never passed from the fact that she *chose* to stay with him. My mother chose a husband who was abusing her daughter over the wellbeing of her daughter. Perhaps it's closer to the truth to say that she preferred protecting herself from a fear of the unknown, protecting herself as a weak woman, over the wellbeing of her children.

My mother treated Christianity like a buffet—take what you can use to your benefit and leave the rest. She would go on to say, "Jesus Christ has forgiven him. And so have I." You have heard that sentiment before. In the proper context, I can see its pertinence. . . . In one nine-word sentence, she had not only killed my faith in Christianity, but my faith in her as a mother. Then, she one-upped herself. When I plead to my mother for help, she responded that I was ruining our family. Imagine saying that to your daughter while knowing full well her husband had put his penis all over her. According to her logic, I was not only a home wrecker, but I was not a very good Christian, either. I understood religion was her "thing," but wouldn't her religion have, at least, dictated she kicked his ass to the curb? I think the adultery commandment should have covered what he was doing with me. It was one thing when she didn't know what was happening. I had kept that secret for so damn long, finally tried to tell her, then still got brutalized. *Then,* when she finally believed I was telling the truth, she still allowed him to stay. Every fucking night I had to sit at the dinner table and look at them both. The disgust I felt was worse once she fucking knew. My mother had forgiven him and blamed me. She told me the "right" thing for me to do was to forgive him. Years of therapy haven't helped.

I never could understand her thought process. Even after all of these years and all the grueling hours of therapy, part of me is still so angry that she stayed with him until the day he died. I never understood why she stayed with him. I never figured out if she was a product of the times or if she was really that desperate to "keep up with the Joneses." Our family wasn't rich by any means, but as long as we no longer lived in an apartment and she didn't consider herself dirt poor, her integrity and protecting her daughters were secondary concerns. Sadly, my mother had been for sale to the highest bidder. One doesn't make the wisest decisions when they're abandoned at the age of twenty-eight, with four children in tow and one of them is a newborn (me) and has two failed marriages to her credit. I guess it's fair to say that, at that point, she was desperate. Clearly. For her desperation, my mother got a corpulent pedophile with a bad comb-over for a husband, but at least he offered her security. Most men want a beautiful woman, and most women want security. The combination can make for a perfect match, and this was WAY before match.com. Jim was able to take my mother to expensive restaurants with names he couldn't even pronounce. Twice a year, just the two of them went on vacation. How fortunate for her that she was able to sell her soul for a cruise, a trip to Barbados, Hawaii, Europe, and Aruba.

I simply can't understand how any mother, least of all my own, would choose a sick fuck over the health of her children simply because she didn't want to be alone. She wanted her material life intact and didn't think about what was on the inside. To my mother, what others would see or perceive was all that mattered. Just like the Olan Mills portrait at the beginning of this chapter and that horrid, fake bookshelf background, fake was okay as long as it appeared to be real. Truth be told, everything in that photograph was fake. It's supposed to be a "family" picture, but the picture is missing my older brother. A "family" portrait isn't a "family" portrait without all your children there. Any normal mother would prefer a picture of her and her four kids, but it didn't matter to Mom whether there was one kid or four in the picture. She was more concerned about having "him" in it. So, we took the family portrait anyway. We look like one big, happy family, but it is a false representation of a much darker reality. The smiles, the happiness, the "family," the background, are *all fake*. Don't let that cheesy smile on husband number four's face fool you. Behind that smile was always a hand grabbing an ass— mine, my sisters', even our friends. Always wanting to do much more to me. He was a perverted alcoholic and a pedophile.

The pedophile passed from pancreatic cancer in early 2010, right after I turned forty-one. I'll never understand why he couldn't have been stricken with pancreatic cancer thirty-five years earlier. I couldn't help but fantasize about how my life might have been so much less painful if he had. When he passed, my mother was suffering from Alzheimer's. After the death of the molester, also known as husband number four, my brother and I were trying to determine the best course of action for my mother. It was very difficult to determine the best options for a woman whom I so despised, yet who needed my help. My compassion for an aging woman trumped any meaningless lesson she ever taught me. My brother and I ended up moving our mother out of the home she and the pedophile had shared for twenty-five years.

During the process, we found all of the love letters between our natural parents from the early '60s—letters written by a young man so clearly in love with this woman so many decades ago. It was the only bit of affirmation of their love that I had ever seen or felt. It was clear the pain of him leaving had been more than she could bear. For the first time in my life, I could actually feel her pain. For years, she persisted with her pain, along with never ending comments about what a loser my father was. It was painful to hear, and it went on for *years*. Granted, he never stepped up like a father should. It shouldn't have been difficult to send a birthday card and a Christmas gift once a year. He managed to show up on those days, but the weeks in between were often silent. The silence was deafening for a young girl who simply wanted her father to love her, but my dad was never going to be considered for father of the year. My mother's rage toward my father would continue for years. I *completely* understand the pain she felt, but will never understand her lack of rage for the man who molested her daughter.

Some lessons my mother taught me were invaluable. I have to admit, she did teach me how to hold a fork. Having been on a few dates with guys who couldn't properly hold a fork, I truly appreciate that simple lesson. *What a turn off.* My mother taught me vanity, too, but that's a double-edged sword. Health is, no doubt, very important. Good looks are a secondary benefit to taking care of oneself. I always say I'm too vain to be a drunk. Alcohol is full of empty calories; it will quickly help you to put on the pounds, and I have no interest in being a fat drunk. It's just not a good look. When you're 5'2," seven pounds can make a big difference and look like twenty pounds on a taller person. Tragically, my mother also taught me zero compassion for other people. Painfully, that's a lesson so deep within you that you simply can't just pull it out of your ass when it's needed. She would always choose men over her children. Always. Even after the birth of my own children, I had to endure that man. I have so many stories to tell, but this is no Stephen King 700-page horror novel. It's simply a memoir with parts that read like a horror story. This is more of a *Reader's Digest* version of my life and my mother, but there are pivotal, life changing moments with my mother.

In 2015, I was fidgeting (as usual) on her floral, Ethan Allen couch. Everything in her house was perfectly placed. A picture-perfect home full of expensive, branded, material things that hold enormous dollar value but zero emotional value for me. Her jewelry and collectibles, alone, were most likely worth more than the suburbanite tract home where she was living. I glanced over at the refrigerator in the kitchen with its linoleum floor and cringed when I saw a red, heart-shaped picture magnet. The magnet's frame held a picture of my mother and the now-dead child molester. I was so annoyed by this cheap magnet because it was being used to hold artwork on the refrigerator created by my son. *My* son, my fourth, my last, and my baby boy, Robert. His sweet, innocent young hands had created an endearing piece of art. Robert's masterpiece was being displayed by a picture of the very man who had shoved his penis down my throat. Robert just happened to be eight years old at this time—the same age I was when the abuse started.

Boy oh boy, did I lose my shit. I snapped, I cracked, and that was it. I couldn't take it. I stormed over to the kitchen and removed the magnet from the fridge. I broke the picture of the "sweet" couple, with so many dark secrets, into as many pieces as I could and smashed the magnet all over the floor. Then I immediately marched my furious ass up the stairs in search of the 8x10 picture of *just* him, so beautifully framed and matted. I took the picture, frame and all, into the garage and *smashed it* with a hammer into a million tiny pieces. Next, I stormed out of her house with smashed, heart-shaped magnet in hand, leaving my mother crying in the kitchen.

I had no idea what *she* was crying for—was it for my lost childhood or the epically bad decisions she'd made all these years? I wanted to believe her tears were for me. I wanted her tears to be for my anger, my sadness, and all she had allowed me to endure at the hands of this horrible man. But I was too afraid her tears were for her dead husband, so I dared not ask. Perhaps it was something as simple as the fact that I had left an awful mess behind. Her mantra was always, "Cleanliness is next to godliness."

When I got home, I realized that the not-so-heart-shaped-anymore frame was still in my hands. Little Richard, my oldest child, and fifteen at the time, came to me with a very worried expression and asked, "What's wrong, Mom?" I showed him the frame with the smashed-up picture, and he promptly took it from my hands and burned it in the kitchen sink. As he lit the picture and frame on fire, all I could think about was that he wanted to protect me. This was such a surreal moment for me. My *son* was protecting me in a way my mother never did. I couldn't analyze it too much in the moment because I needed to take it all in. To really take it in. At the time I thought I felt liberated, but I later realized I actually felt vindicated by my own son. My *liberation* came the day my molester died, and, on this particular day, I felt vindicated.

I knew it was time to talk. And I mean *talk*. Real talk to anyone who would listen. And I mean anyone. From this point forward, the narrative that is to come won't be pretty, but it sure as hell is going to be honest, and, hopefully, funny, and certainly poignant at times. Some of you will relate, some of you will get upset, and some of you will judge me and think I'm nuts. You'll have to take a number on that last comment. No doubt, I am nuts. The stories to come will detail a woman going through a massive transition: from a monotonous, monogamous decade in her thirties, raising babies, to a wild, pill-popping, oversexed, fucked-up, selfish ride in her early forties, to a woman coming full circle and, for the first time in her life, coming of age in her fifties. Now, it's all coming to a stop—not my life, but the pain, the pretending, and the guilt I was forced to live with, yet never had a choice in creating. There is no use numbing myself anymore. Joan Rivers said it best: *"Can We Talk?" Oh yes we can.* We're talking *right now.* If I can help even one woman (but hopefully many more) to understand they're not alone, then I'll know I've been through hell for a reason.

My therapist once told me we are all nothing more than a result of our upbringing, that our subconscious minds rule us, no matter what. How we are raised, what we deal with as children and even teenagers, will render our results as adults. Well, SHIT! That's pretty scary for me, but then she continued to tell me our subconscious minds can be altered, too. The subconscious mind is merely a software program that can be re-programmed as adults, provided we actually do something to remove all of the viruses. Lord, I have a lot of viruses that need to be removed. My therapist also stated that, in some cases, it could make us rebel against our parents, but we do have the ability to go either way—negative or positive. I think I chose both routes. I chose the path less traveled. I sure as shit wasn't going to follow in my mother's footsteps and become reliant on a man, and I sure as hell didn't want to relive my childhood over and over again by putting my children through the same hell I endured. I am truly grateful for my strength.

My childhood is the foundation for my way of thinking. My experiences would drive me to want, need, and desire my own money, my own intellect, my own independence, and to create something more for myself. I aspired for so much more. There's nothing like a childhood filled with sexual abuse, rejection, zero affirmation, and very little, if any, affection to make you desire more. What an awful start to my life. I know I'm not the only one who has not only experienced this shit storm of a childhood, but I had four selfish people steering the ship. Anyone who has lived this nightmare has more questions than answers. I did learn, though, at a very young age, to *never* settle.

I didn't know it at the time, but this atrocity would create a detour in my life that has taken me down many roads: good, bad, crazy, indifferent, intelligent, and stupid at some points. *Finally*, it has taken me here and has made me an advocate.

A sexually abusive stepfather.

CHECK ✓

A mother who was never present.

CHECK ✓

A father who rejected me.

CHECK ✓

A stepmother who was . . . well, just plain pathetic.

CHECK ✓

What does all this mean, anyway?

Chapter 6

Passing the ACE Test
with an F

"All my life been running from a pain inside me"

—"Fear," Blue October—

One of the ways I have learned to understand my mess of a childhood is through a test created in the 1980s called "The ACE Test." I think it's so relevant in understanding any childhood—including mine. It puts the hell I endured in perspective by explaining how those childhood experiences made such a powerful impact on my life, from my teenage years to my adult years.

What is the ACE test anyway?

In 1985, in San Diego, Kaiser Permanente did a public health study to pinpoint diseases in obese patients before the symptoms appeared so they could tackle the problems. In doing so, they hoped health care costs would ultimately be reduced. They surveyed more than 17,000 (17,421 to be exact) members of the program. And what did they find? Adverse experiences in childhood are very common. Across the board: all races, all socioeconomic classes, all levels of education, and even in the white middle class part of the US. That would be me. Thus, the Adverse Childhood Experiences (ACE) test was born. If you want the full details of the study by Dr. Vincent Felitti and his team, please read the article written by Jane Ellen Stevens.[3]

I found this study to be a fascinating read. The questions start with the subject of obesity. Dr. Felitti found out childhood trauma often leads to obesity as adults. For these patients, over-consuming food and the inevitable outcome of obesity was a means of protection against depression, anxiety, intolerable levels of fear, and, yes, unwanted perpetrators. As one raped woman said, "Overweight is overlooked, and that's where I need to be." *Wow.*

But the study evolved to a much larger mind shift. We now understand that so many of us who score highly on this test have turned to a wide variety of addictions to cope. What's

---

3. https://acestoohigh.com/2012/10/03/the-adverse-childhood-experiences-study-the-largest-most-important-public-health-study-you-never-heard-of-began-in-an-obesity-clinic/

your addiction of choice? Alcohol? Opioids? Cigarettes? Sex? Food? Thrill sports? I've tried *all* of them. What about you? Please, God (whom I don't fully understand), please help to stop the anxiety, fear, hate, anger, and, yes, the depression, even if my health is at risk. I'll do what it takes. But it's not just addictions we *choose* to engage in. It can be far worse. We can be susceptible to a multitude of chronic diseases, too.

I took the test to better understand the effect of my trauma. The test administrators asked some really very simple yes-or-no questions, all related to my childhood. Questions related to experiences that were grouped into three sections: household dysfunction, abuse, and neglect. Checking "no" on any question yields a zero for that question, and checking "yes" yields a point. The highest possible score is ten. God forbid. But it does happen.

Any way you look at this test, I have both failed and aced the ACE test. I mean, sixty percent on any test is a big fat F. My score on the ACE test was a six out of ten. I have failed very few tests in my life—there was that F I got on my federal taxation final in college, but come on, have you ever really read, much less understood, the tax code of the United States government? Yeah, me either. Oh, well. I wasn't meant to be an accountant, it seems. Clearly, I thought I failed this ACE test. I soon found out not only did I *not* fail, I *passed with flying colors*. But this was not a test I wanted to pass.

Here are the ten questions on the test:

1. Before the age of eighteen, did a parent or other adult in the household often or very often swear at you, insult you, put you down, or humiliate you? Or act in any way that made you afraid you might be physically hurt? (*Emotional Abuse*)

2. Before the age of eighteen, did a parent or other adult in the household often or very often push, grab, slap, or throw something at you? Or ever hit you so hard you had marks or were injured? (*Physical Abuse*)

3. Before the age of eighteen, did an adult or person at least five years older than you ever touch or fondle you or have you touch their body in a sexual way? Or attempt to actually have oral, anal, or vaginal intercourse with you? (*Sexual Abuse*)

4. Before the age of eighteen, did you often or very often feel that no one in your family loved or thought you were important or special? Or your family didn't look out for each other, feel close to each other, or support each other? (*Emotional Neglect*)

5. Before the age of eighteen, did you often or very often feel that you didn't have enough to eat, had to wear dirty clothes, and had no one to protect you? Or your parents were too drunk or high to take care of you or take you to the doctor if you needed it? (*Physical Neglect*)

6. Before the age of eighteen, were your parents separated or divorced? (*Household Dysfunction or Divorce*)

7. Before the age of eighteen, was your mother or stepmother often or very often pushed, grabbed, slapped, or had something thrown at her? Or sometimes often, very often, kicked, bitten, hit with a fist, or hit with something hard? Or ever repeatedly hit over at least a few minutes or threatened with a gun or knife? (*Household Dysfunction or Mother treated violently*)

8. Before the age of eighteen, did you live with anyone who was a problem drinker or alcoholic or who used street drugs? (*Substance Abuse*)

9. Before the age of eighteen, was a household member depressed or mentally ill or did a household member attempt suicide? (*Mental Illness/Suicide*)

10. Before the age of eighteen, did a household member go to prison? (*Incarceration*)

Simple enough. Ten short and to the point questions. Let's do this. Let's answer these as honestly as possible. I told you I'm the lucky winner of saying yes to six of these questions about my childhood. Yes, that's six out of ten. Can you guess which ones? If you've read the first part of this book, it's easy to identify a few of them. Clearly, sexual abuse is at the top of this list.

But what about the other nine questions? Divorced parents. That's two points. Throw in some emotional neglect from my mother. When she tells you that you're ruining the family because her husband abused you, I'm guessing that number four above—did your family support each other—goes out the window. Now, I'm up to three points. The number you don't want to hit is four. There was substance abuse: oh, how my step-father loved that vodka. There was always a bottle in the freezer. He always had a glass of vodka at the dinner table. He even always had a glass on the bedside table. Wonder if he would chug some with his orange juice before he made his way to my bedroom at 6 a.m.? That motherfucker was a huge drunk. Oh hell. That makes four "yeses." So, from age seven on, I lived with a rotund, combover, speedo wearing drunk. Fuck. This scenario puts me at serious risk for a life of addictions. But, I'm not done with this test: number nine above—mental illness. Unfortunately, the sick fuck of a pedophile did not kill himself, but my mother suffered serious depression. Like a functioning alcoholic, she was a functioning depressed woman. She always went to work, but when she got home she went straight to bed. I'd be depressed, too, if I had to come home to that combover, fat fuck. Up to five "yeses." Halfway to a perfectly fucked-up and trauma-filled childhood. However, I was never physically abused. Unless you count being spanked with a belt, a brush, a wooden spoon, or a hand. Those were generally a pop on the ass to autocorrect my behavior, but they were few and far between. So, I'm going with a "no" on the physical abuse. Thank God.

Which of these is the last of the horrid experiences I endured? My mother would NEVER let a man hurt her physically. I'll give her credit on that one. She was far too vain for that to happen. When it happened to her sister, she looked down upon her sister. Seriously, she had the gall to judge her for being a victim of physical abuse, when your husband was fucking your daughter? She is one judgmental bitch. Then, when the abusive husband of her sister committed suicide, she ran to support her. While she was gone for three days, her husband had his way with me. All weekend long. But, hey, you look good for being there for your sister.

So, that leaves two more ACE questions. We were never physically neglected: we were always fed, and we always looked the part. Being healthy was part of that. So, that leaves one last question. Incarceration. Sadly, both of my brothers spent time there. What they did was their own doing. What led them there . . . well, I'll let all four of their parents answer those questions.

Thank God that's over. No more questions, please. I can't handle it. I scored six "yeses" out of ten yes-or-no questions on the ACE test. So, what does that mean? It means good luck with living a healthy, addiction free life. The odds are truly against you, even *exponentially* against you.

There are a few unfortunate facts about the results of ACE test's original 17,421 participants:

1. 2/3 experienced one or more types of adverse childhood experiences. 87% of those had two or more types.

2. Two out of nine people had an ACE score of 3 or more, and one in eight had an ACE score of 4 or more.

3. 75% were white, 11% Latino, 7.5% Asian and Pacific Islander, and 5% were black. They were middle-class, middle-aged, 36% had attended college and 40% had college degrees or higher. The average age was fifty-seven.

With four or more "yeses," the risk of medical, mental, and social problems as an adult greatly increase. Compared with people with zero ACEs, those with four categories of ACEs had a 240% greater risk of hepatitis, were 390% more likely to have chronic obstructive pulmonary disease (emphysema or chronic bronchitis), and a 240% higher risk of a sexually-transmitted disease. They were twice as likely to be smokers, twelve times more likely to have attempted suicide, seven times more likely to be an alcoholic, and ten times more likely to have injected street drugs. In addition, they were more likely to be violent, to have more marriages, more broken bones, more drug prescriptions, more depression, more auto-immune diseases, and more work absences. I'm more likely to be raped later on in life. And nearly well over 90% of those with four or more are on some type of prescription anti-depressant medication. Now *that's* depressing to me.

So, how does all this trauma affect us at fifty, landing us in the hospital so many years after the abuse? Ahhhhh. *Too much stimuli and too much hormonal release* can physically damage a child's developing brain. DING. DING. DING.

The bell has just rung in my head. In more ways than one. Consistent spikes in hormonal release at a young age can become toxic. Remember emotional Amy, our almond shaped amygdala in the core of our brain, where we store our fear, our love, our hate, and our innate need for survival? Yep. She needs to grow at a normal pace. She doesn't like too much at once. Too much cortisol, too much adrenaline, too much dopamine, too much oxytocin gravely affects her. Yes, I said *gravely*. With a score of 4 or more (remember, I have a score of 6), we are *twelve* times more likely to have attempted suicide. I have NEVER actually attempted suicide. But the thought has crossed my mind more than I want it to.

I can throw stats at you all day long. The doom and gloom is depressing. I now know the odds are stacked against me. Is there any hope in all of this? Should I just throw in the towel now? Say fuck it? What's the point? Is my entire life going to be lived in constant fear of the molester coming into my room to have his way with me? And why did I actually let it happen? I was eight years old, and he was the only adult in my life who showed me an ounce of affection. My dad had left, and my mother didn't even know I existed, except when she wanted to show off my perfectly prim and proper hair and coiffed dress to the other Sunday church-goers. What a sick competition from that woman. "Look at me. Look at my children. See how beautiful they are?" But him? He showed me intimacy, albeit in a sick, perverse way. But it was all I knew. It was all I ever got. And that is fucked up, and I'm more confused now than ever. Does sex mean intimacy? Where is healthy intimacy? I was both afraid and welcoming at the same time. Do you have any idea how hard this is to admit this in writing?

I—we all—need hope. I need to know I'm not going to be an eternal mental nut job. I need to know I can have normal relationships with men. And women. I can't trust men, and now I realize I can't trust women. With so much toxicity in me, I'm destined to live a life in constant fight or flight mode. From eight on, I realized I was living in a world of constant fear and worse—guilt. It's no wonder I drink, smoke, and engage in risky behavior—both sexual and non-sexual. I'm going to need to choose a better lifestyle if I have any hope of actually getting the fuck out of here. Which way do I go? What road do I take? Overachiever or underachiever? Or maybe the middle? If I let this ACE affect me so gravely, I will end up in the grave way too early.

But *wait*. There's another test out there. It's the Resilience Test. This test was developed in 2006, in Augusta, Maine by health advocates of Southern Kennebec Healthy Start. It's another simple test with only fourteen questions created by two psychologists, Mark Rains and Kate McClinn.[4] *Yes!!!* When I first discovered the Resilience Test, I felt a massive amount of relief. I thought, "Maybe I'm not completely doomed." It shed some light on my past and how it relates to my current life. There are ways I can improve my chance of a fulfilled life that doesn't end in suicide. It's a good thing because this "6" score on the ACE test is really gnawing at my soul. Like a woodpecker pecking away at that tree. Peck. Peck. Peck. So fucking annoying. Will it stop? Finding out about this test gave me some hope at a decent life. Somewhat. Maybe I'm not destined for a life full of addictions. Or am I? Which will I choose? And, thus, comes the fork in the road. Now, if I can just develop trusting relationships, be positive, ask for help, seek the comfort of other adults who a) don't want anything from me for their own personal satisfaction and b) don't ignore me because I'm too much of a burden. If I can be resilient, I just may find hope in all this.

This Section's All Yours
Making Sense of Your Childhood Trauma

At the close of each section, I've put together these sections to prompt reflections on similar experiences you may have shared. Some reflection prompts are activities, my self-composed handy "how-to" guides, or simply questions for you to answer whenever, and wherever, you can.

---

4. https://acestoohigh.com/got-your-ace-score/

Let's start of on a positive note. What's your resilience score? What's mine? This is merely a guide to prompt reflection on those experiences that may have protected us from perps in our lives.

RESILIENCE Questionnaire[5]

1. I believe that my mother loved me when I was little.
   ❑ Definitely true   ❑ Probably true
   ❑ Not sure   ❑ Probably Not True
   ❑ Definitely Not True

2. I believe that my father loved me when I was little.
   ❑ Definitely true   ❑ Probably true
   ❑ Not sure   ❑ Probably Not True
   ❑ Definitely Not True

3. When I was little, other people helped my mother and father take care of me, and they seemed to love me.
   ❑ Definitely true   ❑ Probably true
   ❑ Not sure   ❑ Probably Not True
   ❑ Definitely Not True

4. I've heard that when I was an infant, someone in my family enjoyed playing with me, and I enjoyed it, too.
   ❑ Definitely true   ❑ Probably true
   ❑ Not sure   ❑ Probably Not True
   ❑ Definitely Not True

---

5. https://acestoohigh.com/got-your-ace-score/

5. When I was a child, there were relatives in my family who made me feel better if I was sad or worried.
   ❑ Definitely true ❑ Probably true
   ❑ Not sure ❑ Probably Not True
   ❑ Definitely Not True

6. When I was a child, neighbors or my friends' parents seemed to like me.
   ❑ Definitely true ❑ Probably true
   ❑ Not sure ❑ Probably Not True
   ❑ Definitely Not True

7. When I was a child, teachers, coaches, youth leaders, or ministers were there to help me.
   ❑ Definitely true ❑ Probably true
   ❑ Not sure ❑ Probably Not True
   ❑ Definitely Not True

8. Someone in my family cared about how I was doing in school.
   ❑ Definitely true ❑ Probably true
   ❑ Not sure ❑ Probably Not True
   ❑ Definitely Not True

9. My family, neighbors, and friends talked often about making our lives better.
   ❑ Definitely true ❑ Probably true
   ❑ Not sure ❑ Probably Not True
   ❑ Definitely Not True

The Shelf Life of a Secret

10. We had rules in our house and were expected to keep them.
    ❑ Definitely true   ❑ Probably true
    ❑ Not sure   ❑ Probably Not True
    ❑ Definitely Not True

11. When I felt really bad, I could almost always find someone I trusted to talk to.
    ❑ Definitely true   ❑ Probably true
    ❑ Not sure   ❑ Probably Not True
    ❑ Definitely Not True

12. As a youth, people noticed that I was capable and could get things done.
    ❑ Definitely true   ❑ Probably true
    ❑ Not sure   ❑ Probably Not True
    ❑ Definitely Not True

13. I was independent and a go-getter.
    ❑ Definitely true   ❑ Probably true
    ❑ Not sure   ❑ Probably Not True
    ❑ Definitely Not True

14. I believed that life is what you make it.
    ❑ Definitely true   ❑ Probably true
    ❑ Not sure   ❑ Probably Not True
    ❑ Definitely Not True

How many of these fourteen protective factors did I have as a child and youth? (How many of the fourteen were circled "Definitely True" or "Probably True?") _____

Of these circled, how many are still true for me? _____

NOW YOU GET TO WRITE ABOUT YOU

I'm definitely not the only one who suffered from hurt and abandonment in childhood. If you picked up this book, I'm guessing parts of my story may be familiar to you. Consider these questions and reflect—to yourself, in these margins, or elsewhere—to help begin the healing process.

1. Who was it in your life who abandoned you? Mom? Dad? Older sibling? Family member? Some other adult?

2. Were there adults in your life who hurt you, physically, emotionally, or spiritually?

3. What was shoved down your throat? Religion? The push for perfection? Were there other things that had no business being there?

4. To put it delicately . . . who fucked you up?

5. When you think about the traumas of your childhood, how do you feel?

6. How have those traumas affected the choices you've made and the life you've lived, all the way up to today?

7. In what ways have you shown resilience?

Part 2

Numbing Myself through Overachieving, Marriage, and Having Babies

•

My Teens and 20s

Chapter 7

An Overachiever
in the Making

**"She's a good girl, loves her momma.
Loves Jesus and America, too."**

—"Free Fallin'," Tom Petty—

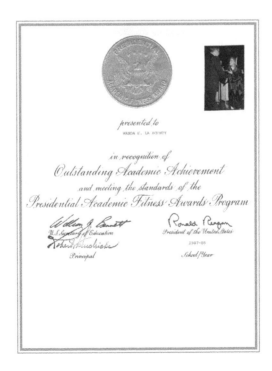

presented to

WANDA E. LA ROOSITY

in recognition of

Outstanding Academic Achievement
and meeting the standards of the
Presidential Academic Fitness Awards Program

William J. Bennett
U.S. Secretary of Education

Ronald Reagan
President of the United States

Principal

1987-88

School Year

I was ten years old and thoroughly confused. I just wanted to be normal. Fuck. What does "normal" mean anyway? Fortunately, Kentucky made its way to our rearview mirror, and we moved back to Texas in the summer of 1980, just in time to enjoy that summer heat wave. One-hundred degrees for forty-two straight days. I'd take that heat any day just to avoid the semen running down my legs again. As soon as we made it to the Lone Star State, the abuse stopped and I could finally breathe. Luckily, the pedophile's new project had him on the road five days a week, I finally felt freedom, and I soared in my own little niche of my small outer world. I had no choice but to create my own happy place—but he was still there in my world. Now, I had to choose which road to take after the molestation with a mother in denial and a father who was too busy raising another family. My mother and her husband provided a home and nourishment for my body, but it was up to me to nourish my soul or let it remain deprived. Which path would I take? Would I harm it or love it?

It would be years later that I would come to wholly understand the need for self-love. In my preteen and teenage years, I would do my best to give myself the love I clearly wasn't getting from my parents. It wasn't conscious at the time, but it was the path I chose. In seventh grade, I started playing school sports. For the first time in my life, I played volleyball, basketball, and ran track. I had no idea how good I was at sports because I hadn't played them competitively before, but I excelled at all of them.

Thank God I was a natural athlete because sports gave me a much needed outlet and saved my vanity . . . wait I meant sanity. At one point in the seventh grade, I was the only overhand server in Plano, TX. My first taste of winning the big trophy was that year when we won the volleyball city championship. We actually won a trophy earned from hard work—not given simply because we showed up. Of course, my mother barely showed up to any of my games, since she was too busy dealing with her own depression.

At the end of my freshmen year of high school, we moved two states over: from Texas to Arizona. Anyone who has moved in the middle of high school knows how gut-wrenchingly lonely it can be, and Lord knows I couldn't count on my mother to be there for me. I used to scrape quarters together so I could call my friends back in Texas on the local pay phone. I would have had my ass whipped if I used the home phone to make a long distance phone call. Luckily, I was very resourceful at finding quarters. I was so lonely those first months after I had left all my Texas friends. I still don't understand why my parents wouldn't let me call my friends from the home phone, but it wasn't allowed. Social media would've been such a wonderful tool back then, but there was no such thing. I was NOT entitled. I did as I was told. The saddest part for me was when my sister—my only ally—moved back to Dallas. She was only in Arizona for a few months. With no father to rescue me, no mother to rescue me, and now no sister to rescue me, I was so alone.

I couldn't wait to become part of a team. The loneliness of the move subsided the beginning of my sophomore year when volleyball started. I made friends quickly. One of my greatest strengths was, and is, my ability to easily make friends. Thank God I always had them. This was one of the benefits of my choosing to play team sports. As the setter on the team, I was like the quarterback of the team. I had finally found a home in Arizona. Volleyball would be my sport all the way through my senior year, when I earned Honorable Mention for the All District Arizona team. I remember being speechless, realizing six years of hard work had truly paid off. My achievement had been simply consistency, determination, and hard work. Plain and simple.

Of course, my mother didn't bother to come to many of my games. I can't begin to tell you how many times I would look up in the stands, searching for her face. What a waste of my time. Maybe this is why I still look up in the stands when I play hockey, looking to see if they are there. "Come on, Wanda. You are forty-eight years old. Nobody gives a shit about over-forty-chick-league-hockey, and your mother with dementia, who can no longer drive, and your father doesn't give a fuck." I just don't get why I have such difficulty processing this. Amy, who invited you to this chapter? Go home.

Sports kept me sane. Sports made me feel part of something much larger than myself. Over the years, I had some impressionable coaches who made me feel like I belonged there, like I was wanted, like I was special. And the coaches didn't have to touch me inappropriately to make me feel special. *Finally. Normalcy.* It had only taken a decade and a half to get there. Thank you to Coach Benge for making me feel normal, wanted, and special. Thank you. My teams became my family: I had teammates who counted on me, and I counted on them. Being on a team and playing sports were my only coping mechanisms, and thus my only hope of surviving without my friends from Texas. I've always told my children that you have to be part of something bigger than yourself because that means they have to be held accountable for something other than their damn iPhone. All four of my children chose sports, thank God.

Thank God for friends and athletic ability.

Not only did I choose to excel in sports, but I put my nose in my books and made really good grades. I knew in the back of my mind that a top-notch GPA was my way out of this hell, so I made the honor roll and the Honor Society. I was number forty-seven out of eight-hundred kids, which put me in the top seven percent of my high school graduating class. I received many honors for someone who felt no honor in her personal life. Oh hell, my accolades gave my mother plenty to brag about, which is ironic as well as immensely annoying.

During those years, the only place I found freedom was when I went to a small camp in East Texas. From the ages of six to sixteen, I spent every summer there for two very short weeks. It was away from home and away from my predator—therefore a much-needed break every summer. I loved Camp Langston. It was the good part of my youth. Better yet, it was the great part of my youth. It was the *safest* part of my youth. I don't know where I would be without it. *Nobody* ever touched me inappropriately there. *Ever.* After my parents dropped me off, I could literally feel the freedom. I felt like I could finally breathe. Have you seen an electrical storm fly across the sky on a warm, breezy summer night? It was East Texas' version of waves coming ashore. Simply mesmerizing. Have you seen a rainstorm run across a lake? More importantly, have you ever gone skinny-dipping in a lake under a moonless night, with the sky blanketed by millions of stars? Have you ever felt such freedom at such a young age? Especially when your home life was painful beyond words?

When I turned sixteen, I made the best possible choice for me: to become a camp counselor—to help and guide the younger campers so they may have the same kind of pure, raw fun that I had each summer. I couldn't be certain if any of those kids had been sexually abused, but I could only assume that many were. It's a numbers game: statistics tell us three to four girls out of ten will be sexually assaulted by the time they are eighteen. So, in six weeks, with one-hundred girls every week, the numbers were there. We didn't talk about it—we didn't have to—but I was there for them. And for me. For their peace of mind. For my peace of mind. For their freedom to simply be a kid. For my freedom to be a kid. Every summer from sixteen to twenty-two, I felt true liberation.

Outside of camp, it was the '80s and I was thriving. Who doesn't love shoulder pads, bright colors, and Bon Jovi (even though "86 it" meant to trash it)? I was finding some semblance of success: post-molestation, post-exposing all, post-my mother's denial. Outside of my many homes, I managed to keep it together. Straight A's (well . . . mostly). Honor roll student. Varsity athlete. Fun. Lots of friends. I was a really good student—until junior year, when the underage drinking began. Because that's what everyone did, right? Have you ever partied in the desert, with the police paddy wagons and helicopters looming overhead and around the corner? Why do sixteen-year-olds engage in underage drinking or engage in sexual behavior when they clearly aren't ready? Why risk so much for so little gain? Luckily, most of the time, I was smart. I chose to limit my questionable behavior and make better, more solid decisions. I kept all the deviant behavior in check. I rarely drank, and when I did, it was on the weekends with my friends. I almost never drove after drinking, but Uber would still have been great back then. Even a cell phone to call any sober person to drive would have been great back then. We made sure we always had a quarter on us, just in case. I never got an MIP (minor in possession of alcohol) or a DWI. Thank God. I know plenty of people who did, and I saw what happened to them. I used to say the only difference between us was that they got caught and I didn't. Lucky, indeed. Maybe I didn't engage in that risky behavior enough to get caught. Clearly, I understood it only takes one time to get caught, but sometimes life can simply be a numbers game.

Part of this '80s bliss was from my friendships. Years before WTF lit up every text on a regular basis, my best friend from high school, Kristina, used to say it all the time. She would pick me up every Saturday in her kickass 1985 black Toyota Supra. Kristina loved to plow past my driveway, knocking the trash can over. I'm sure it was to get attention from the child molester mowing the lawn in his blue speedo (I get that Arizona is hot year-round, but come on. Nobody, and I mean *nobody*, wants to watch a fat fuck mowing the yard, wearing a banana hammock with an enormous gut looming over it. Least of all . . . me!). As she would pull up in her car, I was always so happy to see her. After all, her car was way cooler than the piece of shit Chevy Chevette I drove. Her car had an actual AM/FM stereo, with four speakers, whereas my "Shitvette" had one speaker, with a factory installed AM radio, with an FM adapter I bought at Kmart. Her Supra had electric windows, whereas you had to crank my windows. Her leather seats were way more comfy than my vinyl, and the tires on my car were so small my friends used to say the tires on their mountain bikes were bigger.

I wasn't allowed to do anything with anyone until my chores were done each Saturday. That meant I had to vacuum the entire house, dust everything, and clean the bathrooms—and if my mother was in one of her really foul moods, I had to iron the child molester's dress shirts. I became really good at getting stuff done quickly. I couldn't wait to get the fuck out of there. We would go to the local drug store every Saturday morning to buy what seemed to me to be an endless amount of unnecessary make-up. I could not have been more of a tomboy, and she could not have been more girlie. We were exact opposites, but I'd never had such a good friend.

I don't remember actually telling Kristina about my abuse, but I remember she always made me laugh about it. What other choice does a high school kid have when her stepdad is baring all to the world? They say laughter is the best medicine. Thank God she was able to help me find the humor in just about everything. We've been friends for over thirty years because she made me realize I'm fucked-up, but at least we can still laugh. She gave him his nickname of "Speedo." Well said, girlfriend! Thank you for helping me to find the humor in my fucked-up childhood!

She was the first person I shared my story of abuse with other than my mother, but Kristina actually believed me. What a tremendous relief for me to have someone finally believe me, yet not shove some unusable and meaningless Bible verse down my throat! Kristina's loving, Latin mother, Yvonne, used to go off about my stepfather. I finally had a family who believed me and felt I was able to have some justice in this world. They took me under their wing and always welcomed me into their home. I have no doubt that I ate everything in their fridge. For the first time in my life, I finally felt I had a home. I felt safe there. I had people who not only believed me but loved me and made me feel safe. And where else could I get guacamole on Thanksgiving?

Their love and care for me helped me to understand the Resilience Test from the last chapter. Due to this family's interest in me, I was finally able to experience some of the love and stability a family is supposed to provide. I've stayed close to Kristina to this day, and I stayed close to her mother until her untimely passing in the mid '90s. I still remember thinking when I heard about her diagnosis, "Why her? Why not the pedophile?" After all, he had already paid for college, had served his purpose, and the world would've been a much safer place with one less pedophile. Yvonne, on the other hand, was a lovely woman, deserving of a long and blessed life. Yvonne was so important to me, she was like the real mom I always wanted. Plus, I had my first tequila shot with her, and she drove a 911. Her parents were the coolest couple, and I adored them. No matter how bad your home environment is or your circumstances are, someone else will take you in and make you part of their family. This is a big part of the reason why my house has always been the "Kool aid house" for my children and their friends. I want it to feel welcoming and safe to these kids because I know how much it means to me.

Still, throughout all of the highs of my high school years—the volleyball wins, the parties, the Saturdays with Kristina—the pedophile was still in my world. My mother paraded her known-pedophile husband around all of my high school and college friends, as if he were some prized trophy. I don't know about you, but I prefer my prizes to be worthy, or at least not wear a speedo—but I'm a complicated woman. So much of my confusion with that man is that HE raised me, not my father. HE paid for college. HE bought me my first car. HE paid for my braces. HE went to my high school graduation, when my father couldn't be bothered to actually show up and be present. HE presented me at my sorority's pledge presents. Fuck. Did I actually just give him credit for doing all those things? HE also molested me.

It's so difficult to understand all of this, as I still can't stand him. I can't stand what he did to me, and I certainly can't give him credit for helping me become the person I am today; however, he was the one who was present in my life. He financially supported me all the way until I graduated from college. I kept my mouth shut then. Looking back now, I wonder if the reason I kept it shut was to NOT stop the money train. I knew I had to graduate from college to get out of my environment. My college diploma was my ticket to freedom, and I understood that all too well.

Chapter 8

An Entire Decade of Diapers, Breastfeeding, and Pregnancies

"Our hands are full, but our lives are empty . . ."

—"Sleeping at the Wheel," Matchbox Twenty—

"Your father will *not* sit in the front row of the sanctuary with me and my family."

Word for word, that's actually what my mother said to me at my wedding, but only after I won the epic battle of which of the two lessor evils got to walk me down the aisle. Twenty-seven years had passed since my father had left my mother, and she was still throwing a temper tantrum about it. Talk about being stuck in your own emotional abyss, aka your amygdala. It was 1997, and I was beginning what would be a seventeen-year journey in marriage. There was no way in hell I was going to let the child molester walk me down the aisle. No fucking way. My mother threw a fit—like a spoiled child not getting her way. There is no *fucking* way she will let my father sit in the front row with the rest of my family, much less next to her, *because he cheated on her and left her.* However, she was more than happy to have the man who sexually molested me sit next to her, beaming with pride because she won the battle.

So that's a good thing, no? I'm starting my wedding off, delighting in the victory over my mother versus being blissful on my wedding day. The battle of "the lesser or two evils." It's not like my father was the grand prize, but he did have amazing ice-blue eyes, jet-black hair, and was in incredible shape, versus the potbellied, combover pedophile. Now you tell me: who would you prefer to give you away at your wedding? Remember, looks in Dallas count for everything. Sorry, combover dude. I'll be damned if any fat fuck walks me down the aisle. Add one to the win column for Wanda.

The pedophile, though, was seated next to my mother, and the man who left her was seated behind her. Apparently, there's more to be said for a loyal man than a cheater, but I would have to count unwanted sexual contact with my daughter as cheating in my marriage, so I'm still grappling with that one. Yes, Jim stood by her year after year and never left her. What a lucky woman to have such a high-quality man at her side for so many years.

What a cluster-fuck of feelings I had. I was so excited, so in love, and so ready to marry this man. The church was beautiful, and all nine bridesmaids looked stunning. They were all dressed in classic, full-length black dresses. My future husband and his groomsmen looked dashing in white tie and tails. The whole event was all very black and white. Even all of the roses were white. Looking back, the message I was sending was clear: I'm as black and white as they come. No "fifty shades of grey" with this woman (not yet anyway, but keep reading!). It was a huge wedding, held in the second largest Methodist church in the US, and the place was packed. Everyone was there to celebrate this marriage. My father was standing next to me for one moment in time, and I felt so proud to have him there. I knew I wanted to build a relationship with this man, whom I never got to know. I wanted him to be proud of me. "Look, Daddy. I made a great decision. I'm getting married, and my future looks bright. *Maybe* my family will have the chance our family never did. *Just maybe.*"

I smiled so widely, so genuinely when I saw Richard, my soon-to-be husband. Like any bride on her wedding day, I was both nervous and excited. Then, as I walked down the aisle I saw my mother to my left—with my abuser sitting right next to her. Still, I knew I'd won. I'd forked out tens of thousands of dollars of my own hard-earned money to have *my* wedding *my* way. The only thing I didn't pay for was my wedding dress, which I believe was a Vera Wang. Labels have never been important to me (other than the pink-stitched Gloria Vanderbilt jeans I had to have in sixth grade), but they mattered a lot to my mother. Therefore, she was willing to pay for my dress. My father was there with me, and the molester did *not* give me away, as she'd wanted. I was so proud to be moving on with my own life. There were over 500 people there to honor us. It was overwhelming, to say the least. I had an image to uphold, so organizing the wedding was a tremendous responsibility. I was definitely marrying "beyond my means" and, yes, the pun is intended. My guess is Richard was marrying me because I was lively, attractive, and could spawn him some beautiful babies.

It was hard for Richard, my fiancée, to understand my abusive background as his existence had always been so far removed from any sort of sexual abuse, trauma, or harm. Odd as it seemed, Richard knew no other way than to see a father walk his daughter down the aisle at Highland Park United Methodist Church. Highland Park Methodist is one of the largest Methodist churches in the country and was President Bush's church when he lived in Dallas—our minister officiated at the morning-after service in the National Cathedral, for the

Presidential Inauguration. It was expected for me to have my father walk me down the aisle at our very formal wedding.

I should have known, though, when I had to plan the honeymoon, that I would be planning every detail of our married life together. I met Richard two years prior to the month we got married, and I loved the way he made me laugh. He always had a great story to tell, but after hearing the story about wrecking Rod Stewart's Lamborghini for the fiftieth time, there's only so much a girl can take. Let's face it, it's just the evolution of marriage: you ultimately run out of material. Even with the four human beings we created, one would think you'd have an endless amount of material—endless stories, new beginnings, essentially, ways to make each other laugh. Yet, we still ran out of material. I still got bored, and it was no fault of Richard's. It was years later that I would learn through a psychiatrist that children who experience sexual abuse have a constant need for stimulation, for endless material. Remember our good friend "Amy" the Amygdala? She loves stimulation, and her growth depends on the amount of stimulation you give her. Once she's no longer given the stimulation she so desperately needs, she no longer knows how to act. If the stimulation isn't coming from positive sources, you'll get it from negative sources because it is still very much needed, like a drug addiction. When your first dopamine high comes at eight years old, you learn to sustain during the dull moments, even though your brain is constantly yearning for that next dopamine high. The fact that I stayed in a seventeen-year marriage is astonishing and speaks better for Richard than anything I could say. As much as I'd love to blame him, I simply can't. It's not his fault that my brain (my Amy, God love her) is in constant need of stimulation.

Richard was, and still is, well connected with a laissez faire, laid-back attitude; a kind, giving soul, but like all men, he could be short-tempered. When you have a one-year-old who needs a diaper change and a three-year-old who is screaming, "Daddy, take me outside to play," you'll lose it on occasion. I will say, I was delighted to see the first time Richard had to change Lizzie's diaper. He was horrified and uncomfortable, too afraid to touch those parts that really needed to be cleaned out. He wanted nothing to do with it. Then I realized how grateful I was I obviously hadn't married a pedophile. Oh, the joys and rewards in life we dare not take for granted.

From the ages of twenty-nine to thirty-six, I basically stayed pregnant. I was a dutiful wife and did everything that was expected of me. I was on autopilot. I had always known I wanted to have four children. My entire thirties were spent being pregnant, breastfeeding, and changing diapers. I felt if my parents hadn't chosen to have four children, I wouldn't be here—even if I had been conceived as the result of failed birth control. My mother spent her entire twenties doing exactly what I did in my thirties, although she didn't breastfeed any of us. She smoked during all of her pregnancies except for when she was pregnant with me. Back in the '60s, mothers would spend a week to two weeks in the hospital after having a baby. Just imagine that. Now that insurance companies have taken over, we do drive-thru births. For the birth of three of my four children, I was given an epidural, but not for Emma, my third.

It was the day before the Fourth of July, and I was ready to have Emma. Having been pregnant for eighteen of the past twenty-two months was killing me. Back to back pregnancies were finally taking its toll on me and my back. Wouldn't twins have been easier? You know . . . like a two-fer? No, not for me. I was desperate to get my baby out of me. A four-month reprieve simply wasn't enough, especially considering it was right when I picked up my new obsession for playing ice hockey. I'm going to go out on a limb and say that contact sports probably aren't the smartest thing to do when you're pregnant. But, then again, I've never exactly followed the rules. That brought me Emma, my little firecracker.

Emma wasn't due for another week, but I was over it. I decided to test an "old wives'" tale and consumed nearly an entire bottle of castor oil. Oh my God, the taste was so incredibly rank. I'll never forget that taste in my mouth. I finally decided to go to bed, praying this trick would work. I should have fully understood what I was putting in my body *before* I made the decision to put it there. What I didn't quite understand—as I was downing the entire bottle—was that castor oil is a laxative. It's not like I had any castor oil just lying around in my medicine cabinet. I had to actually get in my car and go buy it at the CVS just around the corner from my house. The pharmacist was looking at me like I was a nut job, and not just any nut job. I was a nine-months-pregnant nut job in the middle of the night, in the dead of summer heat, in Texas. Do non-Texans really have the ability to fully appreciate and comprehend how miserably hot it truly is in Texas in July? One-hundred degrees feels like one-hundred-fifty degrees when you're pregnant. Weathermen always say, "Well, with the wind chill, that fifty-degree temperature really feels like thirty degrees." Pregnancy temperatures are the opposite. Can you see the weatherman saying, "Well, the pregnancy temperature is actually fifty degrees hotter than what the thermometer says." Summer pregnancies are insufferable.

On July 4th at 3 a.m., an intense contraction was the alarm clock that woke me. And then another, and then another, and another. Then they stopped as suddenly as they had started, thank God. Once I realized I could still actually breathe, I had just turned over to go back to sleep, when I realized I had to go to the bathroom. Argh. The constant need to go to the bathroom in the middle of the night is just part of being pregnant. When I discovered this wasn't going to just be a pee, I settled in for a number two, but it became clear it was going to be a number *three*. It was dark, and I couldn't read the label on the castor oil, at first. I knew this was about to become excruciatingly painful, so I called the doctor.

"Wanda, how far along are your contractions?"

"Ummm . . . every few minutes? Maybe?"

"Okay, come to the hospital. I'm here."

"Richard, get up. This baby is coming!"

Richard called his mother to come stay with our two children, Little Richard and Elizabeth, while we went to the hospital. I was in such severe pain, I barely made it down the stairs. I had to get my ass out the door, or our baby was going to be born at home. Luckily, the contractions had taken a break, and I was able to walk to the car like the two-legged mammal I am. I was driving a Hummer back then they weren't exactly easy to get in and out of when you're little; like me. Being nine months pregnant, made it damn near impossible.

When Richard stopped at a red light, I looked at him and said, "Richard, run the fucking light." I could have killed him at that moment, but I really needed him to get me to the hospital, so I refrained. I don't think Richard had ever run a red light before, but in that moment, he knew he had no choice. I was so grateful it was the middle of the morning on a holiday and there was zero traffic. We had gotten to the hospital in less than six minutes. Damn. It helped he had run the damn red light. I couldn't believe I even had to tell him, but that would be one of those extremely clueless male moments.

As we rolled into the labor and delivery parking lot, I had another contraction. I managed to get out of the Hummer and lie on the parking lot. The contractions were coming quickly, and I needed her out of me badly. So, Richard put it into high gear and got us through registration.

"Social Security number please," Richard looked at the triage nurse and said, "Ummm, my wife is about to have this baby. Can't we do this later?"

A porter with a wheel chair took me to a delivery room about 4:45 a.m. They put me on the bed, and I screamed for an epidural. The panicked nurse refused, saying I was already dilated to a ten and the baby was coming. Luckily, my doctor (and also my soon to be neighbor) was already there, waiting to catch Emma. Nothing like spreading eagle and screaming at the top of your lungs for your neighbor! After Richard finished the paperwork, he quickly came in the room and managed to video tape all of the madness. Whenever Emma watched the video of her birth, she always said, "Mommy, why were you crying so much when I was born?"

"Tears of joy, honey." Yeah, right. It was fucking painful. As Emma was flying through the birth canal, Dr. Richards told me to stop. "WHAT? ARE YOU KIDDING?" I thought I was dying. I had to get the baby out of me. Unbeknownst to me, as Emma's head was crowning, Dr. Richards was unraveling the umbilical cord wrapped around her neck. Meanwhile, her head had stretched me further than I'd ever been—my vagina was burning so badly I was sure someone had actually lit it on fire.

At 4:56, Emma made her way into this world, exactly twenty-six minutes after we had left the house. Note to self: CASTOR OIL IS A LAXATIVE. Not only will it get your bowels moving, it will put you in labor. Consumer beware!

Luckily, I only had to do that drug-free birth one time! I realize a lot of women choose to give birth without an epidural, but once was enough for me, even if it wasn't by choice. I'll put a check in that column. That experience gave me a tremendous amount of respect for women who choose to give birth naturally. When given the opportunity with my fourth, I told myself I could do another drug-free birth; however, that lofty goal ended the moment I dilated to a four. *Oh well. At least the thought was there.*

For most women, the birth of their children is one of the most memorable moments of their life. I know that certainly holds true for me. We all have a birth story to share. Giving birth is the easy part. It's raising them that challenges ALL of us to our very core. One thing I knew for sure about raising kids was there was no way in hell I would emulate my parents. I want to give them so much more than I was ever given, but I don't want them to be spoiled, entitled rich kids. The biggest challenge of my life, thus far, has been raising my children to be decent, empathetic, confident, loving human beings. Not self-serving assholes.

Chapter 9

How Not to Raise Assholes

**"I will never leave her like you left me and she will
never have to wonder her worth"**

—"Piece by Piece," Kelly Clarkson—

My child would never do that . . .

I saw this meme on Facebook, and it really made me think. Where does the liability fall on children's behavior? You've heard parents who say, "My child would never do that." Can I get an eye roll, please? I'm calling bullshit.

What they're trying to say is, "I didn't pull that trigger," but the truth is that they raised him to that point. What he does from that point forward is his doing, but what he did up until that point WAS your doing. If you never had your child take ownership of their fucked up moments, how will they ever take ownership over anything as an adult?

You know you have friends who have said, "My child would never do that." Perhaps even you have said it. But me, I can't ever remember saying this. I am the first person to look them in the eye and say, "What the fuck did you do?" In my house, you are guilty until you are proven innocent. I'm not one to hold back. In life, in parenting, in dating, and in my blog. I can't tell you how many times my older daughter, Lizzie, has said to me, "Mom, do you have to cuss?" Yes. I'm an adult, and I choose to cuss. I know I cuss more than most parents, and there's so much controversy today over a parent cursing. What comes out of my mouth doesn't denote what comes out of my character. I'm strong and intelligent, with an excellent work ethic, and I'm certainly not lazy. I care deeply about my children's futures, and I get shit done.

I feel very strongly about both parents taking ownership of their child's behavior. Children will never own their behavior if we, as parents, don't own it first. People say, "Kids will be kids." I say, "Assholes will be assholes." Ask yourself what kind of people you're raising. My goal is to raise independent, compassionate little people, with a healthy dose of self-esteem. Not assholes. Well, Robert, my fourth, is a cocky little shit, but he could be taking after me. Richard, my firstborn, isn't cocky at all. Three out of four isn't bad. I start out great, but my finish needs refinement, and I'm owning up to all that. Perhaps I can make a dent in my kids' lives after all. I'm not one to give up, so I'll keep working on it. After all, Robert isn't an asshole *all* the time. He's as sweet as can be (when he's asleep). He's also very funny, engaging, loves attention, and plays hockey. He's a kid after my own heart. His attempt at the trumpet is cute, at best, but I love that he's trying. At least he's decent on the drums. He's tiny, and that concerns me. Not because I care about appearances, but because society will pull on this kid, and I know how cruel people can be. What he lacks in size, he certainly makes up for with what comes out of his mouth. But, and I mean *but*, it's also up to me to ensure this kid has self-esteem, knows he is loved, and that he's just fine the way he is. Hopefully, that will be enough.

My mother taught me a lot about vanity. "Smile pretty for the camera, Wanda!" Even though I hardly wear make-up today and truly could care less what people think, I do know how to clean up well, thanks to my mother. Outside of summer camp and a hand full of sparse vacations here and there (mostly in the humid South, where it's impossible to maintain good hair), I was never truly able to experience much of the world. In essence, beyond my mother's cherrypicking parenting, I was left to raise myself. Whatever judgment I had—be it good, bad, or indifferent—it was all about performance-based acceptance in our house.

The result was a foul-mouthed, honest to a fault, complicated me as a mother. Perhaps, instead of cursing so much, I'll aim for two octaves less than my normal scream level. That's more doable. I'm rather content just being me. Knowing what I do about bad parenting because of my parents, I changed up the game for my own children. Suffice it to say my parents were weak people, which thankfully did not rub off on me. They had an excellent work ethic, and I'm grateful that rubbed off on me. I'm grateful my mother taught me manners. Brash as I am, I do have manners.

I believe it's our job to teach our children manners. Starting with the most simple and basic manners, like greeting another human being. Things like saying, "hello" or "good morning." I kid you not, I have seen children who are incapable of a simple greeting. Worse yet, I've seen them do this in front of their parents, and no one bothers to correct them. So, if a child is incapable of saying hello, then it's a parent's job to teach them. If they can't be bothered to say hello in your presence and you can't be bothered to correct them, then why would you ever expect them to change their behavior? Trust me, people notice. Down the road, when your kid gets busted for something, and your response is, "My child would never do that," I'm quite certain he or she absolutely did that. Because, somewhere down the road, you turned a blind eye, didn't correct him or her, or never made them own up to their own behavior.

I also believe in spending a lot of valuable time with your kids and their friends. I've had a lake house for ten summers, and we've always had friends and their kids stay with us. Our motto was, "the more, the merrier," but with all that "fun," came a lot of "work." Getting there and getting back home was intense. Loading and unloading the car is laborious. I spent more time yelling at my kids to help unload than I would have if I had just done it myself. Most of the time, kids—not necessarily mine—were eager to help. It's a lot of work for one woman. And then occasionally, you would get the kids who didn't do a thing. They were not good guests. They were more than happy to eat, ride the jet skis, and swim in the pool, but couldn't be bothered to help load or unload the car. Those little shits didn't get an invite back. I didn't understand it at all. I tell my kids all the time to learn the words, "What can I do to help." Teaching your children manners, will render you good adults in the future. When all else fails and you're old and feeble one day, they may come over and say, "Hey, Mom. Can I help you out of that chair?" Teach your children how to be polite, for God's sake.

I do lots of activities with my kids, but I'm not patient. I can only wonder how much damage I am doing to them. If only parents came with an autocorrect function, like the keypad on my iPhone. I feel like I'm walking a very thin line. I want my kids to have what I didn't, but sometimes it's hard to know where to draw the line. My drive, my work ethic, and my incessant need for a better life is so deeply rooted in me, and I wonder if my children will have it. Giving them the gift of time is far better than any material gift, but if you're giving them the gift of time, it should be more quality time.

When your kids do offer to help, make sure they understand it's just as important to get off their ass and actually help. We should teach by example. We need to follow through; otherwise, our words are meaningless. We all want our kids to be decent human beings. We all know kids aren't perfect, and that's probably because they're just mimicking us. If we can't be bothered to correct them, then who will? I certainly don't want to be that parent in denial. Don't be that parent afraid to correct their kid. Your children are a reflection of you. I am extra tough on my kids because of my childhood, and I am aware of this. I tend to say "no" more than "yes," but my kids have a great life, they are LOVED, and my ex-husband and I are very involved in their lives. "No" means "no," but when they do well and work hard, they get a happy mother—plus some perks.

Highs and lows, sometimes it blows when we screw up, and, occasionally, when we get it right. I'm raising two girls and two boys. They are all very similar in so many ways, yet so vastly different in others. I wouldn't trade them for anything in the world, and I am so grateful I can give them a good life. In terms of parenting, I'm the first to admit that the word "challenging" doesn't even apply. It's *taxing, exhausting,* and *fulfilling* all at the same time. Joining Cirque du Soliel would be easier for me: I feel like I'm balancing on a high wire most of the time, with my kids, and I'm ready to drop at any moment. We all feel that way, at times. So many personalities, so little time to figure them all out. But we do try because we are parents. It's our job and our passion, too. I don't want to raise assholes.

My oldest son is a responsible self-starter: very independent and intelligent, with great confidence. My oldest daughter works hard, makes great grades, and is loved by many, but she's my child who has been most affected by the *material* things around her. It's a nightmare. She wants to "keep up with the Joneses" and would rather impress others than herself. I pray, pray, and *pray* she grows out of it. My second youngest, Emma, is as compassionate as they come. She absolutely loves dogs. I've never seen anything like it. She's so kind and defends the weak. She wants to make sure everyone is okay. Emma does have serious test anxiety, so we'll work on that, but she has compassion beyond the realm of human conception, and I'm all good with that. She has a slight competitive streak—perhaps that will prevail as she gets older. Then, there is my youngest. My little boy. He's my doppelganger; my mini-me.

He's a verbal little shit with awesome athletic skills, but that little boy is pure love. He will come into my room and kiss me on the cheek. Most parents put their kids to bed, but he puts me to bed and makes sure I'm okay. Robert is such a sweetheart. I hope that aspect of his character never changes, but he's a small child, and I worry about that. Still, it's my duty as a mother to give that kid self-esteem. I always say that the two best gifts we can give our kids are an unyielding empathy for others and a healthy dose of self-esteem. Four kids with four totally different personalities and one ME!

My youngest child, Robert, loves to snuggle with me. He won't admit to it and only does it when no one is looking, but he does. I take to the fetal position when I go to bed and, he snuggles right up next to me. I hardly don't exist any other time during the day, except when he wants a new game for his Xbox or for me to make him yet another bowl of Ramen noodles. He's in his own little world. It will be interesting to see how this kid turns out. On one hand, he *loves* his video games and excels in them, but on the other hand, he's also an athlete. I was very competitive and athletic as a kid, but couldn't play video games to save my life. But then again, I was always trying to run out of the house. I've never given my kids any reason to want to escape me. Perhaps that's the difference.

On the other hand, my eighteen-year-old finally decided to spend five minutes with me. He is so busy with his friends and his travel schedule. Thank you, honey, for squeezing your mom in to your busy schedule. You know, the woman who gave birth to you nearly two decades ago. When my sister was in town, she slept in his room. My oldest decided to sleep in my room. Sixteen and willing to sleep next to his mother. I thought back to fifteen years ago. I was excited! *My oldest is going to snuggle with me!* Yeah right. Who am I kidding? He is on the edge of the bed. The other edge. He may as well be in California. For a sweet moment in time, I thought my eldest was going to be vulnerable with his mother. That would be a big, fat NOPE. So, I tell him I love him and good night. That's about as close as I got. He is too old to be vulnerable with his mother, and that saddens me. It seems like just yesterday I taught him how to throw a ball. Well, I suppose eighteen years of yesterdays. By the way, he told me if I was going to tell the world that he was sleeping with me, he was going to have a few words with me. Well, I'll keep that in mind. That's certainly a fantastic way to get his attention and get him to talk to me.

I count my very lucky stars that I chose to have my fourth child. I'm reliving Richard's early childhood through Robert. It can be surreal at times. I have to pinch myself; I see so many similarities between the two of them. I may not get to hug my eldest much anymore and get lots of kisses, but I get them through my baby. Sometimes I forget where I am, I forget which boy I'm watching. It was just seven years ago when my oldest started tackle football. Now my baby is playing football. Luckily, all Little Richard's old gear fits Robert —the helmet, the pads, all of it. No way in hell would my oldest take hand-me-downs. Richard won't even eat leftovers, but not my Robert. The only thing that kid has that's original issue is his mouth guard! He wears his older brother's football gear, hockey gear, and baseball gear. You name it. He wears ANYTHING his big brother gives him and with pride. I love that I get to see those cleats and helmets come out of hiding and have life again. I suppose it's my own version of Ground Hog Day, except I keep getting more hugs. More kisses and more touchdowns to cheer for on the sidelines. I'm a lucky mom. It was worth the last pregnancy, even when all my friends said, "Wanda, you're crazy." Not crazy, just reliving a really good part of my life as a mother with this cocky little aggressive, highly confident kid.

There wasn't much snuggling in my house growing up. There was plenty of molesting and occasionally some snuggling with my mother, but she wore fire-retardant pajamas. They were horrible and scratchy! How ironic, the few times she would try to be affectionate with me, I had to endure scratchy PJ's. I guess they were much like my scratchy attitude and demeanor. I would never raise my kids that way. I may not be a perfect mother and my kids may not be the smartest children on the planet or top athletes, but they are compassionate, empathetic young people. They also try hard, and for that, I am proud. I don't want history to repeat itself. I am truly putting forth a conscientious effort to make sure my kids are raised with love and affection. I sure as shit wasn't treated with love and the right kind of affection. There must be a middle ground. I want them to have love, affection, boundaries, and a purpose. My purpose was to get the fuck out of the house. I certainly don't want my children feeling that way.

My oldest daughter is very challenging in the "how not to raise an asshole" department. I'm quite certain I'm doing a stellar job raising an entitled kid. Once, on yet another trek to yet another fucking away game, I drove an hour to Lizzie's basketball game.

Now, I truly believe the gift of time is far better than any material gift, and part of that time I give is through driving. I easily put 30,000 miles on my car a year, yet I have zero of a commute to my home office. The majority of those miles are from my kids' games, and away games are generally far away. After the game, though, Lizzie had the nerve to bitch at me for taking her to a restaurant that was not of her choosing, proceeded to berate me for not signing her out with the coaches, which meant she didn't have to take the bus home with the rest of team, all while giving me evil looks, as I was doing my damnedest to get us back home at a decent hour. Shockingly, when I asked her to put her phone down and tell me about her day and she refused, I FUCKING LOST IT. I'd had it with her. I'd had it with teenagers, and she was only thirteen! It finally dawned on me that I was raising an entitled brat. It seemed as though I had a little pill in the making, and it needed my immediate attention. I still don't know how I managed to overlook this.

I realize my kids may be jaded from growing up in an affluent area. I knew I spoiled my children, but I never prioritize "keeping up with the Joneses." I mean literally—Jones is my neighbor's last name. I strive and work hard to balance my kids, and it's so exhaustingly hard. Achieving balance can be such a lofty goal. I know I screw up on occasion. Okay, I screw up *a lot*. Although "no" is the most used word in my household, I have given in to their demands. Less and less as I get older, greyer, and wiser, but still, I can be just as easy a pushover as anyone else.

Here is my pathetic logic: I was given very little. Maybe my mother did something right, after all. She ignored me, attended almost none of my games, and gave me *very* little, if anything, emotionally or materially. One year, I did get a pair of Gloria Vanderbilt jeans with pink stitching. Remember those? Everyone had those. I *had* to have a pair, but I had to wait until Christmas to get them. Instant gratification? Yeah, right!!! That term didn't exist in the '70s and '80s and certainly not in my house. Can you even imagine if kids had 35mm cameras these days? If they actually had to wait for each picture before they put it on Snapchat? We would have a war on our hands.

Forget my childhood and its lack of instant gratification.

There is no way to EVER explain that to my children. I had to do chores. I couldn't do anything on the weekends until I cleaned the entire house. I had to do *all* the ironing. Don't get me started on the resentment I have about ironing the child molester's shirts. I only wish he was in them when the iron was hot. My goal is to make damn sure my children don't have a childhood that even remotely resembles the one I endured. Not the really bad parts, anyway. I want them to have a far better life, starting with a childhood full of good memories, which requires me being present, both emotionally and physically. Yet, in the process, I feel as though I may have failed them. I have given them WAY too much. Perhaps, even too much love and attention, if that's possible. If I have given them too much, how do I undo what I have done?

There's so much to ponder about being a mother, but maybe I'm being too hard on myself. Maybe it's just their age. Teenagers can make life miserable, and with Lizzie now in high school, I'm hoping it doesn't get any worse. I can't take anymore eye rolls. Of course, I rolled my eyes at my mother, but mainly when she would sit in the child molester's lap at the dinner table. I still cringe at the thought of that. That's an eye roll well deserved. But when my daughter rolls her eyes at me because I tell her to put her phone down and talk to me, it is not deserved. I mean, c'mon, at least my eye rolls were legit.

There has to be a middle ground between what I went through as a kid and the way I am raising my kids. A middle ground where they aren't abused by a man I bring home, and they appreciate everything I have given them. These are things I never had. Where is the middle? Trust me, I'm struggling to find it. If you know or have any insight, please call me on my cell directly. I need help. You thought this was a self-help book. 1-800- HELP-WANDA. The four people I requested to accept me on Snapchat have declined my offer—that would be my four children, by the way. There you have it. In baseball terms, that means I'm batting zero. I'll never make it to the majors batting zero! Whatever happened to your children having to live their lives around you, and not the other way around?

Let's all step up and be parents to our children; otherwise, they will end up being assholes. I know we all agree there are enough assholes in this world already. Seriously, I would love to have a conversation with moms out there about how they are handling our "modern day" children. How do we keep them from being inconsiderate assholes? I would love your feedback.

There is the proverbial scale of judgment, from 1-10. If I were to judge my mother on that scale, she would get a 3.5 on her best days. Now, ask someone how they would judge my parenting on that scale. Personally, I would give myself a 7.5 overall as a mother. Sometimes I earn a near perfect 10 and sometimes a perfect 2 when I need to check out. This could easily be a survival mechanism instilled in us. I still believe one should be checked in when you're with your kids, though. So how do we judge? Or better yet, WHY do we judge? Is there perfect parenting?

Personally, I believe the word "perfect" should be stricken from the English language. No one can live up to this. According to Webster's, the definition of perfect, as an adjective, is "having all the required or desirable elements, qualities, or characteristics; as good as it is possible to be, as in 'she strove to be the perfect wife.'" Are you fucking kidding me? When was this written—1880? As a verb, "perfect" means "make (something) completely free from faults or defects, or as close to such a condition as possible." No one can live up to those standards, certainly not in parenting. I'm opting for the verbs.

But we all still ponder where we are as mothers. Where am I on that scale, or better yet, what would my grade be on a report card? I constantly screw up as a mom. I'm often short-tempered, irritable, and clearly, I'm outnumbered. I'm the only adult in the room most of the time. I'm constantly questioning myself, my actions, and my delivery. I know it's harsh, and I know it's certainly not sugarcoated. I can definitely be rough around the edges. Okay . . . rough is euphemistic. Unbearable, perhaps? I'm sure it depends on whom you poll. Everybody knows I have been known to put my foot in my mouth—a lot! I spanked all four of my children with my bare hand, but never with the things I was spanked with, like a belt, a spoon, or a brush. It's a true wake-up call when you see your own handprint on your child's behind. Luckily, my childrens' spankings were few and far between but still made their point. They are all too old to be spanked now, but I look back and wonder if it was a smart thing or a dumb thing to do. I'm not really in the mood for a debate on spanking. It is what it is and it's all in the past. I do a lot more screaming now, and I'm quite sure that does more damage, anyway. It's hard to estimate the damage or good I am causing them in the moment.

There is a flipside. It's not all doom and gloom over here at our house. After all, I am the fun, athletic mom who is full of adventure. I'm the coach, the teacher (well . . . at least the substitute P.E. teacher a few times at my son's school). I'm the mom who got in the water with all four of my kids and taught them how to waterski. "Tips up!" Oh, the patience it takes to get a six-year-old up on skis. They all did it, though! As they got up and skied in a circle, I would lie there in the water, praying not to get hit by a boat. Talk about scary! I taught all four of mine how to throw, hit, kick, and catch a ball. I got all four up on ice skates. I take them rock climbing, zip lining, snow skiing, and waterskiing. If it involves anything outdoors or on a court, a field, a rink, or a gym, I'm all in. If you ask me to sit and play a video game, I'll fail miserably. Gladly, I was never one to sit inside, as we now know, for obvious reasons.

It's difficult to teach your children things you were never taught. It's like fighting an uphill battle. I'm trying, trying, trying, and I still fuck up. I know I at least get points for trying because participating and supporting your child is essential. I get a 10 on the scale for that. Giving your child love, even when they're driving you crazy, also earns me a solid 10, if we're measuring love. There really isn't a measurement for love. It's just love. What if we gave measurements on a scale for learning and growing alongside our children? There is no measurement for treating your children with respect and teaching them to treat others with respect. Perhaps a more accurate scale to measure our parenting is my version of the Bell curve: the majority of our decent parenting would be in the center of the bell curve, and to the left, would be weaker days of parenting, and to the far right, would be the better, more euphoric moments of parenting.

It is virtually impossible to measure good parenting. I hope you understand that, too. We judge each other on our weight, appearances, social status, economic capabilities, class, intellect, and a veritable feast of other things in life. I hate it, but I was taught that way, too. I am hoping to teach my children how to measure on being themselves rather than comparing. Make a difference. "Don't blend in" is a hard one to get across. Be yourself and as compassionate as you're capable of being at a young age.

At the end of the day, I give myself a ten million on the scale for *not* being like my parents, for breaking the mold on abuse, and for being the best mom I can be, faults and all.

I strive to be present, understanding, and empathetic, which is the hardest thing for me. I am present and I love those kids: that's what they will remember. I raise them to realize they are privileged. I have emphasized just how important it is to go out and help others who aren't as fortunate. To quote John Kennedy, "To those whom much is given, much is expected." It's my job to teach them to be more giving and less selfish. I will fail forward. Hopefully, they will earn a 10 on compassion when they get older, and social media won't screw their little brains too much. Above all, I will make my kids go *outside* and get physical. No matter what happens in life, take it outside—in a rink, on a field, on a court (hopefully not of law), grab a ball and *move*.

Let's not judge each other too harshly, but, if we must judge, then let's judge each other on a Bell curve because it allows for a margin of error. There's always room for improvement. Unless you're a pedophile; then there's no hope for you, and you will be crucified. Having sex with your children doesn't count as quality time. Ever.

This Section's All Yours
Parenting Performance Review

How to Raise Assholes in 10 Easy Steps!

Here are my 10 easy steps on how to raise entitled children who eventually become assholes. You might ask "Wanda, did you really do these things?" Then the answer is YES! I did. Somewhere along the way, I have screwed up. Royally screwed up. I am guilty of doing everything on this list. WTF was I thinking?

3. In what ways do your children surprise you? Inspire you? Help you grow?

4. How do you judge your success as a parent?

5. Is there anyone who has judged you for your parenting in the past whom you need to tell off?

6. What parts of your past most influence your parenting? What parts of your past do you wish didn't influence your parenting?

Part 3

Numbing Myself through Sex, Dating, and "Love"

•

My 40s

Chapter 10

A Haircut, a Preacher, and an O-bitch-uary

"Janie's got a gun. What did her daddy do?"

—"Janie's Got a Gun," Aerosmith—

Even after all that had happened to make me feel abandoned and invalidated by my mother, I was still willing to do anything to have a relationship with her. Since my maternal grandmother died of ovarian cancer in the 1950s, I never had the opportunity to have a relationship with her, but I wanted my children to have the experience of that special relationship with a grandparent. I'm sure I felt this way because some Hallmark card or Lifetime movie swayed my way of thinking, convincing me this was essential to complete the picture of my happy family. Ironically, delusional me was still accepting that the pedophile stepfather was a permanent fixture in my life.

In my early thirties, I hadn't *fully* comprehended the need to keep my infant son away from my molester stepfather. In the back of my mind, I knew never to let Jim babysit Little Richard, but I didn't have a fear of him molesting my son like he molested me in the '70s. My thinking at the time was hopeful. Maybe his propensity for little girls was just a phase he'd gone through in his forties. After downing what must have amounted to an entire distillery of vodka over the decades, surely his libido, and thus his interest in little children, was dead—or so I foolishly assumed. As a grown woman, I know there was no way in hell he'd even try to touch me inappropriately, and I would certainly never let him touch my son. I knew the difference between right and wrong, but my determination for my child to have a relationship with his grandmother would override any thoughts of my childhood experience. I still had such a strong desire to be the dutiful daughter and provide a relationship for my child with his grandmother.

A few weeks after we had just spent the last Christmas of the twentieth century together as a "happy family," Richard and I went to my mother's home with our sweet and very innocent eight-month-old baby, to show off his first haircut. As we were standing in the doorway, I'm beaming with pride, showing off my cute little blonde haired, blue-eyed Gerber baby. All mothers think their children are the most beautiful ever, and I was clearly no exception. In less than ten seconds flat, I went from sheer pride to utter disgust when my stepfather commented, "Your son's haircut is sexy."

What.

The.

Fuck.

I'm aghast, thinking what can possibly be sexy about an eight-month-old, much less his haircut. Then it dawned on me—once a pedophile, always a pedophile.

Since then, I've done a lot of reading on the subject of pedophiles and child molestation. I've come to realize that pedophilia is not curable. In some respects, it's considered a sexuality in and of itself. Some of us are heterosexual, some of us are homosexual, some of us are pansexual, and, tragically, some "humans" (notice I didn't say "us") are pedo-sexuals, who feel they have rights in this world. They have gone so far as to try and attach themselves to the LGBTQ community, and so far they have been unsuccessful, thank God. Sadly, it's just who they are sexually; without an ounce of doubt in my mind, they must be stopped. I can't emphasize this enough: Pedophilia is not curable. Just as you cannot "cure" someone of being heterosexual or homosexual, you cannot "cure" a pedophile. In 2009, neuroanthropology.net published an article, "Inside the Mind of a Pedophile," that reported "Pedophilia, like many types of diseases, does not have a complete cure." I could cite numerous published articles on this subject that are all contradictory, but the reality is, pedophilia is not curable. Although this theory is unproven, I'm certain it is accurate.

When the pedophile uttered those words, there went my hopes for a "happy family life" that included my mother being a grandmother to my son. Unfortunately, my mother, who was standing right next to her husband when he made this comment, couldn't believe I was so upset. My husband and I were so upset that we immediately left her house. I refused to talk to her for a month, but, still, I felt sad for her. More importantly, I was devastated for my child and me. Weeks would pass before I would pick up the phone and call her to talk about that inappropriate comment. To this day, I remember her words clearly: "He didn't mean anything by it." After I had made it clear how upset I was, she still defended him. I finally realized I was going to have to accept that, no matter what, she was "standing by her man." No matter what, and I had to accept that dismal fact. I was convinced then that I needed my own section of cards at Hallmark. I knew that epiphany was a bitter pill to swallow, but, still, when my vulnerable self is exposed, my automatic defense is to be a smart ass.

Months later, I called the preacher at the church where I grew up, Grace Presbyterian Church, in Plano, Texas, where both my mother and stepfather regularly attended. I had finally summoned the courage to tell him their faithful servant was a child molester. I further went on to explain that the information I was sharing was first hand, as I was his victim, and I knew Jim was volunteering at his church. I felt it was my *duty* to let the minister know that Jim *SHOULD NOT BE AROUND ANY CHILDREN*. The minister's response shocked me and rendered me speechless. He said I was an angry person and I should seek help for my anger issues, and that perhaps God could help me. Furthermore, he said I wasn't angry with my *mother*, but more so with the sexual act that had occurred so many years ago. *Ya THINK?!*

I was angry with them both. How could this man—a minister—not even get it? If you think I was angry before, you should have seen my face and my reaction in the car that day. I could have chewed through a piece of wood. The minister went on to explain that my stepfather, my molester, was a good man. He was a good volunteer, and the church valued both him and my mother for their dedicated service. I had to wonder whether the minister was equally grateful for their tithing. At that very moment, I promised myself that no matter how I felt, how sad or even angry I became, I would never take my children back to that church.

Well . . . never say never. I eventually made one exception to my "never again" rule. We did go back one final time. We went back to that church for Jim's funeral so that I could see his ashes in an urn. Watching my mother mourn his death, was way more than I could bear. After reading the bland, generic bullshit in his obituary, I decided some of the pertinent details were missing. I crafted a more accurate version of his life, which I present to you known as my "obitchuary."

James Rogers's "BLAND" Obituary
Published in *The Dallas Morning News* on July 5, 2009

Rogers, James Leo October 11 1926–June 30, 2009. Survived by his devoted wife of 32 years, Melinda, son Jimmy, and daughters, Christine and Roberta; 6 grandchildren, 4 step children, 10 step grandchildren and his beloved dog, Pepper. Served in the US Navy during WWII in the Pacific Theatre. He graduated from CCNY with a degree in Civil Engineering. Jim enjoyed many years in service to the Lord at Grace Presbyterian Church. Memorial Service will be held July 7, 2009 at 2 PM at GPC, 4300 W. Park Blvd., Plano, TX 75093. In lieu of flowers, the family requests memorials be made to GPC for Mission Ministry.

BLAH BLAH BLAH BLAH. The man was a pedophile for fuck's sake! Here is how it should have been written:

Rogers, James Leo October 11 1926 — June 30, 2009. Survived by his ~~devoted~~ *delusional* wife of ~~32 years~~ *31 years too many*, Melinda, son (*not of his wife, Melinda*) Jimmy, and daughters (again, not of Melinda), Christine and Roberta. *Okay. Let's pause here a moment. The way this starts out makes it seem that Melinda was the mother of his three children. Ummm. No. Not only was she not their mother, she was a pathetic, half-ass stepmother. Guess she learned that from her own children's stepmother. I think out there somewhere is the '70s guide to being a shit stepparent. It should be noted that he had two other children from his first wife, but we don't know their names because they were adopted by their mother's new husband at a young age. We have no idea why his first wife would let another man adopt his children. He never saw them after that. We don't even know their names. Hell, I'm not sure they even exist, but he said they existed, so we believe him and think it's important any and all children of the deceased should be mentioned in case they may want to come and pay their respects to the man who fathered them and didn't raise them. My guess is his wife at the time saw his unusual "love" of children.* Wink. Wink; six grandchildren (*we would name them but we don't know them because we never met them*), four step children *who he loved, especially, the girls,* ten step grandchildren and his beloved dog, Pepper. *Fuck the dog, though. Nobody liked the damn dog except his wife. She loved that damn dog. She treated him the way she should have treated her children.* Served in the US Navy during WWII, in the Pacific Theatre. He graduated from CCNY with a degree in Civil Engineering. Jim enjoyed many years in service to the Lord, *a phrase which you can only say with a straight face if you say it with the deepest east Texas accent you can imagine,* at Grace Presbyterian Church. *Now, mind you, we called the church and warned them he was a pedophile. Of course, that didn't matter to the minister.* Memorial Service will be held July 7, 2009 at 2 PM at GPC, 4300 W. Park Blvd., Plano, TX 74093. In lieu of flowers, the family requests memorials be made to GPC for Mission Ministry.

In the future, you will be able to sign up online for my webinar teaching how to properly write your dead molester's obituary.

Chapter 11

Where Do You Wear YOUR Scarlet Letter?

"We build it up . . . we tear it down"

—"Pieces," Rob Thomas—

I magine living back in the mid-seventeenth-century Puritan town of Boston, Massachusetts. You've committed adultery and you've been punished very publicly. You get to wear a big, red "A" on your clothes, denoting your affair like poor Hester Prynne from *The Scarlet Letter*. We all had to read Nathaniel Hawthorne's classic novel in high school. After fourteen years of marriage, the Hester Prynne in me revealed herself. Well . . . not exactly. I wasn't locked up for my affair, even though I lived in the Bible belt, but I was shamed. I might not have been publicly shamed, but I certainly was privately. Rather than being sent to a physical prison, I imprisoned myself, deep in my mind. For me, that was far worse. Being alone with my thoughts can be scary because they often feel never ending. My mind knows two speeds: running a thousand miles an hour or shut off completely.

Sex in our marriage, when it happened at all, had become monotonous, rigid, and unfulfilling. I needed an adventure. I made it past the seven-year itch, but couldn't resist the second time that number came around. The entire decade of my thirties was spent either breastfeeding or changing diapers. I was too busy to think about my needs or wants, and, to be fair, the needs or wants of my husband. I had four babies who needed me. When my youngest was entering kindergarten, an enormous amount of freedom was thrown my way. Sometimes, too much freedom is *not* a good thing.

The fall my youngest started kindergarten, Richard and I were redeveloping a piece of land we owned in Austin. Because Austin is a three-hour drive from Dallas, we felt it was best to hire a local contractor to manage the day-to-day construction of the project. The builder we hired was a referral from an old friend of mine. Since Richard was so busy with projects in Dallas, I used my newfound freedom to drive to Austin once a week to meet with the local builder and check on the progress of the project. I had no idea at the time that very soon, most of my thoughts would be consumed by this man. This didn't happen initially, but the more time we spent together, the more enamored I became with him. He was handsome, athletic, and smart, with a gift for challenging my very bored mind. I was hooked and there was no going back to the life I had known before I met him. He provided me with a steady stream of dopamine, and I felt as though he made me come alive. I didn't know I could ever feel this way again. I was one of those naïve assholes who judged other people for having an affair, just like I had judged my own father. Indignantly, I'd think to myself, "There's no way I would *ever* have an affair." It's not like I was on a "Married and Looking" website, because I wasn't. Fortunately, I was not one of those thirty-five million people who were busted for being on the Ashley Madison website.

We had been working together on an enormous, time-consuming project, and we simply clicked. We talked for hours, and my mind was blown. When we were together, my heart raced so rapidly I literally thought it was going to pound out of my chest. I read *Fifty Shades of Grey* (admit it, you did, too) and became obsessed with the idea of our bodies intertwining. First came the "sexting" and then came the phone sex. I had no idea it was even possible to have incredible sex without even touching each other, or without even being in the same *city*, for that matter.

Then, came the inevitable. We had to take it one step further. A simple touch sent tingles up and down my body. I had goose bumps for the first time in years. The first time we had sex was the most powerful I had felt in years. Sex before the molester died had been limited. I couldn't get past my mental block. Sex after the molester died was powerful. I felt free. Free to really feel. I was consumed by the sex—the intimacy, the connection, and the power of letting myself go. There was power in choosing to be *incredibly selfish*. I'd only shared my secret with a couple of my dearest friends, and one had told me to point my moral compass north, but the only compass I had at the time pointed inward.

The physical, sexual part of the affair only lasted for eight weeks. Eight weeks of pure passion, lust, and, without a doubt, the most *liberating* sex of my forty-two years. But it was also eight weeks of deceit, lies, and betrayal. I was thinking only of myself—not of my husband, my children, or of the friends who would later judge me. I had never been so totally obsessed with another person that nothing else mattered, not even my own children. Besides, in my delusional mind, I thought they were safe at school and didn't need me. Tragically, we can make bullshit excuses all day long for our bad behavior, but that doesn't change the reality of the consequences or the damage done. *And there was so much damage.*

After another moment of disconnecting with my wise mind, I contacted my lover's wife via private messenger on Facebook. I chose the day after Christmas to tell this woman, whom I'd never met, that I'd had an affair with her husband, without so much as giving him fair warning. They say to think twice before you hit send. Not only did I not think about the shit storm I had just created, but I fell into a very deep depression. I had fucked up in the worst way possible, on so many levels, and had no one to blame but myself. Not only had I betrayed my husband, now I had betrayed my lover, as well. I could no longer be with either my husband or my lover. I was alone again with my own mind—my own private abyss of a prison—and this was all self-inflicted. I knew after this I could no longer be intimate with Richard. I didn't even know how to be his wife any longer. Still, I knew I had to end the affair; my therapist kept telling me over and over again that a man rarely leaves his wife and children for another woman. I knew there was nowhere for our relationship to go, but, for me, the damage was already done. I knew "he" would do the right thing and not leave his family, so I had to end the affair, but I didn't have the strength to do it. By sending his wife that message, I chose the most cowardly way possible. The sex and passion were gone, but the pain and loneliness stayed behind. My husband and I continued to live together under the same roof, but I was reminded daily of the pain and destruction I had caused. I couldn't go back to Richard or my lover, ever. I went a year without sex, without love, and, sadly, without the feeling of the cohesive family I had spent the prior decade creating, loving, and nurturing.

After months of hell, I decided it was time to tell the kids we were getting a divorce. It was my decision and mine alone. Richard had no other choice but to give in to my decision, even though he fought hard to save our marriage. I didn't. I had already checked out. Once I'd slept with another man, I could no longer be in our bed. First I moved out of our bedroom, then I moved back in to our bedroom and kicked *him* out. It was an utter disaster. The nights I spent crying seemed endless. I couldn't decide if I missed my marriage, my family, or my lover. I was so confused. The only thing I knew for sure was that I couldn't be with my husband anymore. The years we had spent together building a family were so disproportionate to the few months I took to tear it apart. I built a wall around myself that Richard could no longer penetrate. To this day, I'm still trying to figure out what he did or didn't do to push me away.

As we gathered our four children in the living room where we spent so many nights watching our favorite TV shows, we broke the news to them. Sadly, there was zero emotion on my part. *Where is your empathy, Wanda?* I was dropping an atomic bomb on their lives and felt *nothing*. My oldest, right in the middle of middle school anxiety, expected it. My youngest, barely a first grader, asked if we were done, so he could get back to his video games. My third, just starting her last year of elementary school, took it the hardest. She couldn't stop crying, and I wished I had an *ounce* of her empathy. I couldn't have felt more relieved that the part where we had to break the news to the children was over. It's times like these that I want to thank my mother for teaching me how to have no feelings and how to always shift the blame.

An affair is anything but *fair*. It's devastating and ruins relationships that took years to build, but only moments to tear down. I guess the question I have for all of us is *why?* Why do we do it? Is it worth it in the end? A family forever shattered, left behind to pick up the pieces, all because I needed to be loved. I certainly never felt loved as a child—it was rarely given and purposely withheld. *Why did my need for love outweigh the need to love my own children and their father?* How can you give to others what was never given to you as a child?

My husband had done nothing to deserve this disaster, but I wanted a marriage with more passion. I wanted a marriage where I didn't feel like I was doing *everything*. I had a failed marriage, but I *knew* I didn't want a failed divorce. I care about this man's future and well-being because he's the father of my children. I cannot undo the affair I had, but, again, was it meant to be? *It* being the affair, and then the divorce? It being my ability to screw things up? Yes, definitely. We do *deserve* to feel love and passion, but at what fucking cost?

If you're married and going to have an affair with someone else who is also married, the odds of the relationship making it are slim to none. What goes up must come down. That dopamine high you are feeling comes down harder than you expect when you crash and are left to deal with the aftermath of your selfish choices. If by chance you both leave your respective spouses and marry each other, I can almost guarantee that you will wake up one day asking yourself, "What the fuck did I do?" As high as the divorce rate is, it is twice as high for second marriages.

I suppose we all wear a scarlet letter *somewhere*. I'm pretty sure I'm not the only woman who's strayed from a passionless marriage. I so desperately needed to feel something again. I needed to come alive and be invigorated, happy, and satiated. I thought I *craved* him, or maybe I just craved how he made me feel. Regardless, I knew the right and the wrong of what was happening, and, in that moment, I *simply didn't care*. My body and mind wanted to feel this man, to feel every endorphin rushing to my brain, with every orgasm he gave me that fully engulfed my body.

After it ended, I was left to live with the shame, the guilt, and the emptiness, just like Hester Prynne. However, I wear my *SCAR*-let letter on my forehead, my chest, my back, and my mouth. You name it . . . it's all over me. For me, though, the affair was just the beginning of a roller coaster decade.

Chapter 12

Orgasms Are Healthy, Even after Abuse

"When you're alone, do you let go?
Are you wild 'n' willin' or is it just for show"

—"Love Bites," Def Leopard—

An Orgasm a day keeps the doctor away!

I f you're reading this book and haven't listened to my Podcast yet, you should. I love doing my podcast; it gives me a great forum to talk about anything—and I mean anything. After all, it is explicitly rated—mostly because of the amount of cursing. But those "F bombs" are warranted, especially when they are preceded by my weekly pedophile report. I'm probably the only podcast out there that does a weekly pedophile report, and sadly, I never run out of material to talk about. Nobody wants to just hear about child molesters each week, though, so I open up discussion for many topics. If you've listened to my podcast, you've learned I'm a sexual woman, a sexual being, and in touch (pun fully intended) with myself. Not just my *sexual* self, but my emotional self, too. I *know* my body. I know how to express myself in many ways, and I don't hold back. I take care of my own needs. I *enjoy* it. There's nothing wrong with it, and I'm not afraid to talk about it. It's so important to know how your body reacts to certain stimuli, and for you to *not* be afraid to explore it. This is coming from a woman who has lived long enough, and through enough, to have a clear perspective.

After I started my podcast in 2016, I have had friends reach out to me to ask me, "Wanda, I can't have an orgasm because the abuse is somehow still blocking me. How do I get there?" Wow. I can fully understand their challenge. It took me a long time to understand myself—my needs and my sexual desires. My first consensual sexual encounter was when I was seventeen, but I don't remember the actual act at all. We had sex a few times, but I don't remember any of it. Writing this now, I can't remember if he was a good kisser. I remember *him*, though. I loved this guy, or *thought* I did. The only thing I remember physically is that I had never masturbated as a teenager, which meant I didn't understand how my body worked, whether I was alone or with another person.

Going into college, my motto was "so many men, so little time." Making out with guys was my primary curriculum. I was juggling my studies, which were suffering, and I was partying *far* too much. I pledged Alpha Phi sorority, where I formed strong friendships and made lifelong bonds with some truly incredible women. I know this may come as a shocker, but I became extremely active in intramural sports. I'm pretty sure I was one of the wildest chicks in my sorority. In my sophomore year, I had my first deep vaginal orgasm and found a guy I'd end up with for the next three years—pretty much until the end of college. Mind you, at this point, I *still* had never masturbated.

After college, I became financially independent of my parents, when I realized the chilling truth: the pedophile had paid for my education. Thanks, fucker. You ruined my childhood, but may have given me a future by paying for my college. Hope it helped your conscience, but I doubt it. It would be years later, when I had my own children, that I would realize how much disdain and hate I had for my mother and the pedophile. I had finally realized there had been a financial carrot hanging over my head for the past fifteen years. Not anymore. I was finally free of them and their money. The day I graduated, they cut me off financially, and that was just fine with me. I was completely indifferent and on my way to create a life for myself. I felt I could breathe for the first time in my life.

After graduating, I traveled for my sorority as a consultant to different college campuses, going out with my friends, and having a good time. I was boyfriend-free and was enjoying the pre-texting, pre-Tinder, pre-Match dating world.

I finally discovered masturbation, and I *loved* it.

I began exploring my body and testing my limits. Did it have anything to do with my newfound freedom from my parents? I think so. How can I encourage you not to be embarrassed by this act? It's natural, and it's *needed*, yet we're taught that it's bad, that we should be ashamed for doing it. I have an idea where this shame comes from: closeted, repressed people. Maybe it's those same repressed people who feel it's okay, behind closed doors, to have sex with an eight-year-old.

As an adult, masturbation is a *perfectly normal act.* Do you know how many people I know who don't know how to please themselves? It's shocking. It's wonderful, feels incredible, and then you can roll over and go to sleep. Or perhaps have a good cry after this euphoric high! What is there to be ashamed of? It's *your* body, and you can play with it however you want. *MASTURBATE, I SAY!* Please yourself. Have *fun.* Use your imagination. Read *Fifty Shades of Grey.* Do whatever you need to *get your stimulation on,* ladies. It's normal, natural, and feels so damn GOOD! I started in my twenties and am still having fun with it in my late forties.

Enter my mid-twenties, when I met the father of my children. He was such a terrific communicator. We'd talk on the phone for hours. He came from a good family and was a very interesting man. He had a great relationship with his father, and that was the *number one thing* I was looking for in a husband. I didn't want my children to go through what I had gone through as a child. I was determined that I would make *damn* sure their innocence would be left in place, and they could have a wonderful childhood. This man fit the bill.

And so, as you know, I went on to marry Richard, and we had four children. Much like any marriage, the sex was good in the *beginning*, but then it became a business—the business of creating more children. I wanted to have four children. That was my goal. My focus shifted to my children, and we no longer focused on each other. Our marriage was a business, and the love and passion we originally felt in the beginning started to dwindle. As a sexual being, I found ways *outside* of my body to make myself happy. I worked, I bought material things like cars, boats, and a lake house, and, of course, I raised kids. The constant going and going every day wore me out and whittled my marriage down to nothing but the basic courtesies; we were like ships passing in the night.

Ignoring my own, heavy sexual needs and deep, internal emotional needs, reared its ugly head in the end, demanding attention that couldn't be denied. I should've paid attention to that from the beginning, because I know myself. I *knew* I was in trouble when sex wasn't part of my daily equation. Sex with my husband became routine, and I would eventually come to hate the act. It wasn't all Richard's fault. *Absolutely not.* I played a role, as well. I understood this later on when the pedophile had passed away. I felt an overwhelming sense of relief that even took *me* by surprise. With this newfound freedom and understanding, and being the adventurous, ambitious woman that I am, I cheated on my husband. You remember him from the previous chapter? He's the guy who earned me that major accessory: the sweater featuring that large "A"—my very own scarlet letter. But *fuck me, it was great.*

I now have no intention of ignoring my sexual needs. Hell, they say the more orgasms you have, the longer you'll live. It's all about the blood flow and getting that heart rate up— it's good for the soul, the heart, *and* the body. Orgasms are good for both the emotional and wise mind. I have no issue exercising my right as a woman, to thoroughly enjoy myself in a sexual way, either alone or with the right partner. Being sexual is *normal* and highly encouraged in the proper situation. If you don't have a vibrator, get one and don't be afraid to use it. Sex is *not* dirty. And shouldn't be. Even though I was introduced to it at such a young age, I don't let that moment in time imprison nor define me for life. I'm not afraid to be the woman I want to be in a sexual way, and I will not feel guilt nor shame because I simply enjoy sex.

However, I can't be this sexually crazed woman when my children are near. And by near, I mean in the house with me at the same time. I'm just not going to go there. When my children are with me, I'm in Mom mode. Crazy, sexual Wanda doesn't exist. Sex and children don't co-exist. *Ever.* This is what disturbs me about *fucking pedophiles.* They blur the lines so that they can be more easily crossed. I simply don't get it, and I *lived* it. I *wish* it were a blur, but it isn't. Luckily, I can separate sex from children, but others simply can't. Or won't.

Looking back at all this is a bitter reminder of the sexual abuse I endured in my childhood, and the roles hypocritical Christians played in my abuse and my understanding of sex. I just hate the idea of using God as a tool to make someone feel guilty. When the pedophile died, I am *sure* he wasn't met at the pearly gates, with God saying, "Hey, welcome! You repented of your sin, and that's awesome, so come on in!" No *way* that happened. That man is coming back as a cockroach in his next life, just like he acted in this one.

I have news for you. Christ may have walked on water, but he *cannot* cure pedophilia. It's our job as parents to protect our children from pedophiles. Especially known pedophiles. Pedophilia doesn't go away. Many women don't really ever get over the abuse. They go on for years, unable to have a healthy sex life. Some just suffer unhealthy relationships, while some are just downright scared to be with a partner. Some women *do* get over the abuse, and they are able to move on. They can understand that sex with the right partner, or simply alone, is okay. Despite my abuse, I can still have a healthy sex life. I think many can relate to the hell I endured, to the abuse, and to the long-term damage it does to the soul.

I do know that my realization in the importance of taking care of my own physical needs has played a big role in having a healthy relationship with sex. I am an absolute believer in taking care of *yourself* and *your* needs. It's empowering. I encourage you to try it today. Put this book down and get your blood flowing. Just make sure your children aren't within earshot! The rush of endorphins has altered my mind over the years, and the need for the rush has *certainly* gotten me into trouble. But it's also calmed me, at times. Natural endorphins stop pain. I *love, need,* and *crave* the endorphins. I'm an endorphin junkie. I need the challenge every day. From my kids, to my relationships, and right down to the aggressive sports I've brought into my world. Hockey: talk about a challenge! The rush of endorphins, culminated by a need to be aggressive in the rink—to get that puck and score—is hard to beat. It's really not about winning, but the *rush* of winning. But when it's done, there's a moment of humbleness and a letdown because the game is over. Is it human nature to need to feel a rush of endorphins and find ways to release it? I believe it is. Perhaps there are different levels for each and every one of us. Mine is probably higher than most. Oh, how I love the endorphins.

Crying and Releasing Endorphins

I didn't cry very much as a kid, but I certainly made up for it in my forties. We can go from one emotional state to another with a good cry. I mean a *really* good cry. I found some interesting studies on tears. As quoted from the World of Psychology:

People feel a profound difference between happiness and sadness, the body often doesn't make a distinction. Intense situations of any sort can provoke overwhelming reactions. Whether the trigger is a political victory or a crisis, the body produces more stress hormones as part of the preparation for the fight-or-flight response. Tears act as a safety valve by releasing excess stress hormones such as cortisol. If left unchecked, chronic elevated levels of these hormones can cause physical ailments and play havoc with mood. As stress often precedes a good cry, the sense of calm often felt afterward is at least in part due to hormonal release.[6]

In addition, did you know that there are different types of tears? According to Dr. Henry Cloud, there are tears of grief, tears from foreign objects, tears of change, and tears of laughter. The tears of losing a loved one come from excruciating pain, but cutting an onion will also make us cry. Moving, switching schools, and altering our moods all fall under the category of change. *Oh, the tears caused by change.* Then, of course, there are tears of laughter. Those are the best tears! What an endorphin release those tears create. When was the last time you laughed so hard that you couldn't stop shedding tears? It seems like most of my tears in the past few years have come from grief, loss, or pain. I need a good laugh. I need to feel those tears streaming down my cheeks in a good way. I *need* those tears. And then there's sweat.

6. http://psychcentral.com/blog/archives/2012/11/18/the-science-of-tears/

I work out a lot. I get this euphoric high when I'm skating. I love the feel of sweat rolling down my back, chest, and legs after a good workout, which always makes me feel *so* much better.

Orgasm Endorphins

Orgasms. Now *that* is a rush my body craves. A good orgasm after a hangover can make a big difference. My mood is always altered after an orgasm. Have you ever combined all three: a good sweat, a good cry, and a really good orgasm? Surely, most people sweat when engaging in sex, but have you ever *cried* after an orgasm? I can only wonder what those tears look like under a microscope. Would they look like tears of grief, laughter, or change?

I've had *several* good cries after an orgasm. I wonder what prompts me to cry. I simply can't control it. It's just another rush of endorphins in the body. I crave the rush, the natural highs. I'm inclined to steal a petri dish from my daughter's biology lab, so I can grab my tears after a really good orgasm and then rush it to the science lab, to see how much cortisol I released. I find all of this fascinating. How remarkable the human body is: our unique tears, personalities, life experiences, and all that comes with this crazy life. I suppose I'm lucky in a lot of ways, as I've managed to find release for my pain in sports and my voice. I think we should all have a voice, and be able to say what we think and feel . . . within reason, of course.

They say, "The pen is mightier than the sword," so perhaps journaling would help! Or starting a blog. I'm not the type of girl to sit and write my feelings in a pretty, floral-designed, paper-based journal. I tend to be more of a screamer: in my blog, on the ice, at my sons' hockey games, and, yes, in the bedroom, too. Maybe I should title my next book "Scream, Cry & Release Those Endorphins." Imagine how much money the pharmaceutical industry would lose if we indulged in a little more *natural* endorphin release and stopped relying on opiates. I'm thinking that'd be a much better way of life.

Chapter 13

Accepting Second When You Really Want to Be First

"Have you ever hated yourself for staring at the phone?
Your whole life waiting on the ring to prove
you're not alone"

—"Glitter in the Air," Pink—

N ow that you know about my sexual life, it's time to share more about my dating life. Shortly after my divorce, I began dating. I dated lots of men. None really stuck, and then every now and then someone special would come along. Women can be so angry—I can say this from a first-person point of view—and ex-girlfriends or ex-wives can be especially aggressive. I'll never forget the day a boyfriend told me his ex-wife had said to him, "Your new girlfriend's just dating my *sloppy seconds*." I looked at him for a moment, shocked that anyone would even *say* something like that, then I burst out laughing. I thought to myself, "Wow, what an ego on that one!" I had to wonder if that really made her feel better about herself to call her ex "sloppy seconds?" As appalling as that statement is, it was only said to satisfy her ego. I can only assume the motive for her remark was driven by jealousy. I know anyone who dates my ex-husband is getting a *gem* of a man. Since it seems like everyone has an ulterior motive these days, I can only hope that whoever comes into Richard's life will love him for who he is and not his wallet.

Hopefully, her "sloppy seconds" remark made her feel better, but I'd like to think he's a better man for knowing me. Perhaps she turned him into the "sloppy" man she feels he became in their marriage, and won't take responsibility. When we're married to someone, we're responsible to that person. We're *all* responsible to our partners, and name-calling is childish. Knocking someone down and insulting them is usually meant to affect the new interest's way of seeing them. Just because someone is done with their marriage and walks out, it doesn't automatically make their ex undesirable to others. Sometimes, someone else's "sloppy seconds" can bring breath into your world. We all go through life, busting our ass to get to the next level, the next stop, the next whatever. I'd like to stop and simply take it all in, even if it's with someone else's sloppy seconds.

I accepted being sloppy seconds in my dating life, and I'm fully aware that I let it happen. No shock there when my father always treated me like a different kind of a second—a second fiddle. I shouldn't be surprised at all because, in a way, it was all I knew, and we tend to stick with what we know. I finally realized this after dating so many men. Talk about a painfully tough lesson. In school, we are given the lesson then the test. But in life, we are given the test, then the lesson. It's up to me and me alone to stop this pattern. I won't repeat history by abusing my children, so why on Earth would I repeat it by letting a man treat me like second fiddle or a sloppy second? The truly sad part in all of this is I'm not alone. So many of us accept this subpar treatment, but we shouldn't. We all need to realize that when the universe is telling us to NOT accept being treated as though we are second fiddle, we should listen with open ears.

When my father was diagnosed with cancer, I felt I needed to be there for him, but maybe I needed to be there for me, as well. I suppose it was a last-ditch effort to get to know the man who fathered me. Somehow, I found the courage to go sit with him and his wife at the cancer treatment center. As hard as it is for me to keep my mouth shut, I actually did just that. I know what you're thinking, but I *did*. I created uncomfortable, meaningless small talk with him and his wife about her kids and her grandkids. I made the effort to be there even if I didn't really care about those conversations. As I sat with my dad in the cancer center, watching the chemo drip into his body, I can only wonder what it's like to have these cell-killing drugs running through you, killing both the bad *and* the good. This was his fourth round of cancer; the last time was in the '80s. I can only assume things have changed in the cancer world. Luckily, I only inherited his good looks and tanned skin. Okay, the premature grey hair, too, but thankfully, I haven't inherited that dreadful cancer gene.

As I told story after story of *my* kids, they would interject and add stories about *their* kids. As you know from previous chapters, he raised her children and, now, her grandkids. I mean *their* grandkids. Oh, fuck the pronouns, it doesn't matter. The point is, they *both* know all the stories of her kids and grandkids. Bragging, just like two grandparents do, but not about *my* kids. I had to tell my father what was happening in their lives because he simply did not know them. As I watch them proudly smiling at their grandkids' accomplishments, it was all I could do to stay in that room with them and fake my reactions. My smile was hiding my sadness. I didn't know it at this point, but I had actually begun breaking down the barriers of the sadness that I felt in that situation and started gaining strength by being the better person. I know, now, that I've always been second fiddle to my father's chosen family. Yes, I said *chosen*, and I meant it. He may have MADE us, but he CHOSE them. I'm kissing fifty years old, and this still hurts my heart. My kids are second fiddle to them, as well, and that hurts *more*.

What would shock me the most, however, even through all the abuse and rejection of my father, is that the term "second fiddle" actually came from the man I'd been dating for nearly a year. It came through a text, as if *that's* not a shitter, and then the text messages just *stopped*. Whatever happened to Emily Post's rules of etiquette? Use the right fork, put your napkin in your lap, and please continue a text conversation.

I called him out on his lack of etiquette. Why would you send a text message and then not continue the conversation? Or at least have the respect to respond and say something like "I can't talk right now, we'll talk later." So, I went totally old school on his ass: I picked up the phone and called him. "HELLO, what happened to you in the middle of our conversation?" I wasn't at all prepared for his response. "I'm with my number one girl right now (meaning his daughter), and you're second fiddle." Ouch. Okay, I get it. I will always be second to your children, as it should be, but, damn—that was harsh. I know that my father never said that to *his* wife: the proof is in the pudding. That may be a stupid saying, but it is so true. My father would never have had the balls to say that to his wife. He is a puppet on a string, being led around by the nose. I know this, but it still hurts.

Thanks, "boyfriend," for bringing this to my attention. This man was well aware of my past, all the abuse I'd endured, the rejection, and he *still* said those words to me. I had cried to him many times about my father. I want any man's daughter to be first in his life. I understand and support being second in THIS situation. That's as it should be. I've been second fiddle all my life to my father's wife and her family. I want to be first for once. My man knows there is *no* fucking way I'd date a man who puts me above his children—I'd lose respect for him in about five minutes, but his words were really hurtful to me. I had never heard those words from my own father to his wife in my defense, so it was very hard to stomach hearing it from the man in my life, in defense of his relationship with his own daughter—even though I would hate him if he didn't feel that way. It's very confusing, and the struggle is genuine. Children of abuse don't recover quickly. Even with time and creating a positive life for myself, it's still hard to recover from a statement so hurtful. His words felt like a verbal assault. Sometimes, even unintended remarks are emotional triggers, and then out comes Amy again. Amy, that hateful amygdala.

I have finally accepted I will always be second fiddle to my father's chosen family, as much as I have always wanted to be first. Perhaps that's what I'm choosing now, with these men. *Or is it?* I want to be first in my man's life, but not in front of his children. I won't even date a man whose children take a backseat in his life. I should have been first in my father's life, or at least an equal to his wife's children. Oh, the irony . . .

I know from my experience, times haven't changed too much for women, at least from what I can see. There are still a lot of women who want someone to take care of them. Sure, the company of a significant other is comforting—but at what cost? Are you really for sale? I, for one, am not. I thank God for a brain, a good work ethic, and the patience to discern whom I am willing or unwilling to be with. My mother made me feel I had no value, but I would come to realize that I do. I am worth so much and so are you. Dating is one thing, but marriage is another. They say, "Desperate times call for desperate measures!" Well, not when your children are involved. I don't want my children to accept being "second fiddle" to anyone.

I work hard to be a good example and teach my daughters what I believe in. I want them to have genuine pride by being that woman who is smart, attractive, and hard working. I am kind to their father and work hard to make our post-divorce relationship work so my children can grow up knowing love. All I remember seeing growing up was hate and resentment. I wouldn't subject my children to any of that. Sure, we get into our spiffs, but, at the end of the day, they see that we love them and we will work it out. Broken hearts are inevitable, but my broken heart can certainly heal faster than my child's. Seriously, think before you actually commit. Think about your children, you, your future, and the well-being of all those involved, but not necessarily in that order. The last thing any kid needs is to watch their mother go through another divorce. Or a pedophile (just sayin'). I'm aiming for an equal partner in life.

The best advice I can give anyone is to not be so hasty with dating. I know few people actually enjoy the dating game because, let's face it, it's a series of job interviews that ask you the same questions over and over and over. On one first date, I asked if we could go straight to the fifth date because I couldn't take anymore "getting to know you" questions. And, yes, we ended up in the sack that night because it's socially acceptable to have sex on the fifth date. But in the interest of full disclosure, I have had my fair share of one-night stands.

Take the time to get to know your partner. I have a "four seasons" rule because I don't know how anyone can ever get to know someone until you have been with them all four seasons of the year. After this election year, however, I've decided we may need to consider dating someone for at least four years as opposed to four seasons, seeing how some people can be so extreme when it comes to political views and opinions. A partner might hate Christmas, but it could be your favorite time of year: for many people, that could be a deal breaker. Who wants to spend every year with that guy who hates Christmas if it's your favorite time of the year? More importantly, think about your children. It isn't fair to your children to throw a guy into their lives you've only known for a few months and give them an InstaDad. It took my kids a couple of years just to get into a new routine of two homes. We need to let them adjust. You need to adjust. I'm showing my children, especially my girls, how important it is to be independent and *not* depend on a man.

I can't speak for every woman on the planet, but I would rather suffer in poverty with my children and my integrity intact than sell my soul and my body to the highest bidder. I learned the hard way, unfortunately, through a painful childhood, all brought on by my mother who didn't think with her wise mind. I will never be that mother, and I won't be that woman. If I can impart some wisdom on anyone today, it is to encourage you to "create" your own life. There's no shame in working hard and teaching your children *to take control of their own lives.* I'm inspired when I read stories about single mothers who work tirelessly and struggle to give their kids a healthy life. I greatly admire those women. In my own life, though, I'm at a crossroads, and I need to figure it out. Ultimately, there are three lives in every relationship: yours, your partner's, and your shared life together. You have to have all three in any relationship to create balance. I made my displeasure over being told I was "second fiddle" known to my then-boyfriend. He caused such hurt with those simple words sent in a text message. He never said it afterward and was more careful about the words he chooses, and I'm grateful for that. Perhaps that's putting me first in *some* aspects, without his children ever having to feel like they're "second-fiddle." I'm good with that. I love my children. They are first and foremost, crazy beings that they are. Your partner can be first in many ways, but there must be compromise and balance.

Do you see the irony in this relationship? I defended a man I loved, when someone stated that he was "sloppy seconds," only to be called "second fiddle" by the same man. Life just does us that way sometimes. For a woman who's been emotionally beaten up for so long, I know I have to break the pattern of second-hand importance. If I can teach one person this lesson, then I've accomplished a lot. We will continue to get the same lessons over and over again until we stop repeating destructive behaviors. I could've held a grudge, but I chose to communicate like an adult rather than throw a temper tantrum like a child—even though that's what I really wanted to do. That's the difference, though, between Wanda the adult and Wanda the wounded child. Wanda the adult is doing her damnedest to shield the wounded child. With one bad pattern down, there's one hundred more to go. It's a never-ending cycle of learning and growth. The bigger irony in all of those text messages and phone conversations about the "second fiddle" comment" is they brought the epiphany that inspired this book. There had to be purpose to my pain.

I refuse to stay stuck. I have a big mouth and still know when to use it and when to shut it—well, most of the time, anyway! I'll keep my mouth closed and practice my best Emily Post behavior during my father's chemo because it's the right thing to do. Eventually, I'll put my foot down in my relationship and get some resolution. It's a constant balancing act.

Chapter 14

The Lifelong Hunt for the L-Word

"Funny how the heart can be deceiving more than just a couple times. Why do we fall in love so easy? Even when it's not right."

—"Try," Pink—

My entire decade of my forties has brought me one grand epiphany after another. I finally realized that I don't want to be anyone's sloppy seconds nor second fiddle, but, most importantly, I realized that my search to be loved trumps all. Self-love is clearly the most needed love in anyone's life, but I'm still searching for the love of a partner. I'd been married, had my babies and hundreds of hours of therapy. I've been beaten down so many times that I question whether I have the ability to keep searching. Humans aren't meant to be alone in this world. Studies have shown that it's the relationships in our lives that make us the happiest. Money will never buy us happiness; however, it's much more comfortable to cry in a Mercedes. After a few relationships post-divorce, I'm finding more and more things I don't want in a partner. It's amazing how intuitive you become after dating a few fucked up men with a low emotional EQ. I felt like I was ready to get into a fully functioning relationship. *Bring it.* After years of rejection and abuse, molestation and neglect, *I AM READY TO LOVE AND BE LOVED.*

It took me a while to get to this point, though. After an on-again, off-again relationship, I decided it was time to "go out" and have some fun during one of our off-again periods. For ten months, I was chased by a widower—we'll call him Eli. I thought he was probably the sweetest man I'd met in many years. He was always there for me. Eli was kind, giving, generous—as good as they get. He always complimented me and was great at making sure I was taken care of. He certainly had a better moral compass than most. His wife had passed away, after all. I assumed his wife's passing would at least mean he'd be more sensitive. I even told my *therapist* about him, for fuck's sake. That means something, right? I mean, if I'm taking the time to talk to my therapist about you, *c'mon.* I only get one hour a week after all, and she's damned expensive. At the time, I wasn't interested in anything other than going to dinner and having some "stimulating" conversation. My prior x-boyfriend was still in my heart, but my mind was telling me to move on. Eli wasn't the only man I was seeing: I had also ventured into the unknown world of dating sites. I had decided I was a "free woman," in every sense of the word.

Eli and I dated for much longer than most of the men I met on those dating sites. Most didn't survive more than an interview (I mean, date . . .) or two, but, for some reason, I actually *liked* this man. I began to open up and trust him, and that meant a *lot*. After a few short months, he dropped the "L" word, out of nowhere—and, of *course*, it was during sex. At first, I ignored him. Then, I questioned it. "Do I want this? Do I deserve love? Is this something real? How do I do this? Is he the one?" The second-guessing and self-doubt kept my mind spinning. My brain would go like a train without brakes, and then I would head to my medicine cabinet to try and slow it all down. Then I'd remember, "I threw all my pills down the toilet, damn it."

I pondered the idea of what it would be like to love this man, and I actually started to get excited. I told him I was finally going to reciprocate the care he has shown me. It was my turn to step up and be the giver, not just the taker. Just when I thought I could help develop this relationship, I got a text from him at 4 p.m., canceling our date for that Saturday night. *What?* He's *never* canceled on me. Once I finally began to let my emotional walls down, when I *finally* decided to start caring for this man, when I finally opened up and accepted his relentless chasing, he tells me he will no longer be calling, and that it's over. Eli now said he didn't love me, but went on to explain he had to do whatever it took for me to fall deeply for him. He claimed to have read my blogs and knew the pain I was in. He knew the "L" word was a trigger for me, and he knew my weaknesses. He took the opportunity to capitalize on them. Well played, Eli. Well played.

GO FUCK YOURSELF.

Time passed, and I really didn't think much of him or about him. He simply wasn't worth it. Looking back, I realized he was just another victim of time-fill—someone you waste time with, not someone you fall in love with. The fact that I was able to move on so quickly was a clear indication love was never part of the equation for me. Can we *really* tell ourselves to fall in love with a particular someone? I doubt it. Love is felt deep in your heart and soul. It's not a switch you can simply turn on—it doesn't work that way. We need to depend on *ourselves* to complete us—not another person. My lack of self-worth wasn't his responsibility. That's *my* job *and, thus, my* responsibility.

Eli was just one in a string of boyfriends as I tried to find myself. Let me share another story with you of how "love" goes, post-divorce. I think some of you may resonate with this story. Post-divorce, I have been dating and *dating* and ***dating*** and dating. Dear *God*, make it stop. Online dating *sucks*. The lies are nothing short of colossal. Seriously, you could stick Post-It notes all the way to the peak of Mount Everest with the lies on these men's profile pages. But still, I go, because I'm on an adventure! Hey, I'm divorced—I can play. And boy, *did I play.* I was on a seek-and-destroy mission: I was seeking as many men as I could by sleeping with them and destroying myself along the way. I was not ready for a relationship, and with all of my fucked-up-ed-ness unhealed, I was moving and grooving right down the path of self-destruction. But, hey, I was having some serious fun along the way!

Enter the Boyfriend. Christ, where did *he* come from? I was hit upside the heart with emotion. He was handsome, charming, and intelligent—and all with a great body. I could feel him in the center of my solar plexus, from my third eye, down to my root chakra. *Dammit!* I couldn't get enough of him, and that was just from the first date. Trust me when I tell you I kissed a *lot* of frogs before I found my horny toad. God, how I liked this man. I *really* liked this man. Can you begin to imagine how many triggers this set off in a woman who is working so hard to get her past and emotions in check? *Let the craziness continue.*

Ours was one of those instantaneous relationships where our first date included dinner, breakfast, and lunch—in that order. Our second date had me on an airplane. With my raging endorphins, I couldn't stop thinking about him. I couldn't figure out how I went from those emotionless sexcapades, having a different man nearly every night for a week in my bed, to finding *one* man who is now satisfying me on all fronts. For two beautiful, orgasmic, *incredible* months, I was on the East coast with a man I adored. All of my barriers were down, then he *slammed* on the brakes of this amazing experience I thought we were both having.

Let me back up a moment. A very experienced serial dater once told me I needed to sleep with scores of men before I even *considered* a relationship. I didn't *quite* make that number before I met this amazing man, but what I *did* do was share this bit of advice with him the first night we met. I told him he needed to go put a few notches on his belt, in my most sardonic way. At the time, it was me being me. I wasn't emotionally attached to him yet, so "in my mind" I risked nothing. But, after two months of a "serious" relationship, he decided he would take my advice, but lie about it. Can one really recover from so many lies? If a man in your life lies to you, you should kick his ass to the curb, but I didn't. It was my fault that I chose not to show him the door. Why couldn't I have said, "Fuck you! Have a nice life," after the very first time I realized he'd lied to me? I didn't, and I regret that decision to this day. If we allow our partners to walk all over us, trust me, they will. You just can't let them treat you that way in the first place.

I allowed this to happen. This was a result of my addiction, not his. Relationship and love addictions are very *real* addictions. Romantic love is *not*, nor *should it* be, the most important thing in our lives, but when love isn't received from an early age, love will always feel like the missing piece in our lives.

This man constantly gave me mere crumbs, and I hung on ever so tightly, waiting for more. When a man tells you that he loves you after two weeks, don't believe it. Let it grow and mature. Nourish it. If it blooms after a year, then, maybe just maybe, it's love. Otherwise, it's merely a temporary euphoric high. If a roller coaster ensues after two months, get off the ride. Take a step back. Most of us are on our best behavior for the first couple of months. Then day-to-day reality sets in, and those impostors are replaced by the real people. Don't fall in love with an impostor. Wait until the real person comes out, then you can choose to love *that* person or not. I made the mistake of falling in love with an impostor, and I hung on, waiting for that real person to show back up, but he didn't because "he" had never really existed. So, I accepted the mental anguish, but for what? So I could rip him a new one and get even? In that scenario, who exactly wins? Nobody. All that's left is one empty soul that took another down. Neither one of us can undo any of the massive damage that happened.

Another relationship over, and time for another one to start. After constantly flirting with a dad in the neighborhood—which is not a good idea, by the way—we finally went out, and it turned out he was a lot of fun. I mean, *a lot* of fun. When he told me his recent relationship had just ended, I believed him. This was lie number one of many. He told me he was totally hooked on me, that he'd never met a woman like me. *Blah blah blah.* Oh, the lies. Shocker.

At 3 a.m., he was in my bed, and his phone wouldn't stop with calls and texts. Ten phone calls in three minutes. Clearly, someone was trying to reach him. He ignored it all. Should that have been a red flag? Of course! It was his supposed "ex" girlfriend. At 9 a.m., my cell goes off. It was my neighbor. "Wanda, someone tried to break into our house last night. Be careful." Damn. I hate that, especially when I'm home alone. It was just wishful thinking that it was a burglar, though.

My neighbor went on to tell me that the crazy woman kept yelling some guy's name, which just happened to be the same name as the guy who was with me. "I know you're in there," she would scream over and over again. My neighbor told her to get the fuck off of her property before she called the police. The intruder left to get into her Range Rover because my neighbor won't open her door. Wait, huh? Did you say Range Rover? How many burglars drive a new Range Rover? Yep, another red flag.

I asked what time all this happened. You guessed it. The same time his phone was going off. I sent a pic of his "ex-girlfriend" to my neighbor and BINGO—it was her! Shocking! Evidently, she looked into his Uber account and found out where he was. The problem was, she had gone to my neighbor's house and not mine. If you plan on stalking the liar you are dating, make damn sure you have the right address. Details, I suppose. Crazy? Yes, a psychotic moment. *I cannot make this stuff up.* My neighbor said there was a male passenger in her car. I had to wonder if her passenger was a wingman she planned on using to teach her cheating boyfriend a lesson. It would've been disastrous if she was one of those women who immediately blame the girl, and she was sending her Guido after me! After all, he had assured me they were broken up. Yeah, right. I had to wonder what I had gotten myself into this time.

It turned out he had been dating her on and off again for nearly a year. That was according to the mutual friends I asked (we have nearly fifty mutual friends on Facebook—love good ol' Facebook), but not according to him. I swear, I can't win. I may have to start doing FBI background checks on every guy I have a drink with.

I wish I knew what makes guys feel the need to lie so much. He, of course, went on to lie to me, to her, and to himself. Can't anyone just be honest? His lies didn't really bother me; I'm used to men lying to me. I wasn't emotionally attached to this man and was just having fun. Two adults having consensual sex was fine with me, but for his girlfriend, I'm guessing his lack of honesty surely made a difference.

What makes us go crazy enough to go hunt down a man that makes us so crazy? Trust me, I know. I did the same thing to one of my old lovers. Except, I knew where his house was, and I walked in on him in bed with another woman. It was an utter disaster. My mind was not in the right place. Sadly, neither was the woman's who chased me. I actually felt sorry for her. In all her mental anguish over her lover/boyfriend/ex/

whatever he was, she went crazy, and, sadly, *at the wrong house.* He, of course, went on to lie to me, to her, and to himself.

Again, own your story. Whatever it is.

Still, I got into all of these romantic situations because of my need to feel loved in a relationship. The power of addictions can and will consume most, if not all of us, especially with high ACE scores. The higher the ACE score, the more addictions we're prone to have. Please read this link https://www.five-sistersranch.com/learn/what-is-love-addiction/. It gives you valuable insight to determine if you're addicted to love. You may have these same love and relationship addiction issues. These come from traumatic events from your childhood. We have to let go when a relationship is unbalanced, or simply not healthy. Lori Jean Glass is a relationship expert in this subject. She did her best to help me while I was at Five Sisters Ranch for treatment in Northern California. The only time my addictions take a backseat in my life is when reality slaps me in the face. Yes, my children are my reality. They don't need some love-addicted mother neglecting them so that she can get her unmet childhood needs resolved. This is a very real issue.

I find it so ironic that I can be successful at so much in my life, yet such a failure at the same time. I was so strong in every area of my life except for my love life. I am successful *despite* my parents, not because of them, but they're still dangling that carrot. The ubiquitous love carrot that always seemed within reach, but I still couldn't seem to grab. What I'd really like to convey is this: there are no true mistakes when you're trying to find yourself. It's taken me years of work to come to this realization, and, even now, I'm still a little broken. I need mending. I'm not sure it's possible in some aspects. So, these days, I'm looking for the good in me, the good in you, and the good in whatever person I'm choosing to spend my time with. Because *we're all a little broken, aren't we?*

So, if you find yourself in that place where you're constantly picking "filler men" to take up your *valuable* time, it's okay. Remember my suggestion to write everything down? Make sure to write down what you *do* want versus what you *don't* want in a relationship. Make them pass *your* test, not vice-versa.

This Section's All Yours
Sit Back and Take Stock of Your Dating Life

Dating Do's and Don'ts According to Wanda

To help all of you women and men out there discern what is and what is *never* acceptable in dating, I've created this handy guide. This is serious stuff here—I've been through it all. If you're asking the question, "Wanda, did you really do this?" Then the answer is YES! I did. Somewhere along the way, I have screwed up. Royally screwed up. I am guilty of doing everything on this list. WTF was I thinking?

1. Do be honest. If you're married, just tell me. If you claim you're married but separated, actually be separated. You will ALWAYS get caught. Why not start out being honest? It will save a ton of pain in the end.

2. Do be emotionally available. Stop blaming her for everything. Get over her. Move on.

3. Do be ready. I've nursed far too many men who aren't ready. It's not my job to put your books in your backpack and make your lunch. That's my job as a mother, not a girlfriend.

4. Do understand that the opposite of love is indifference. *Not* hate. Learn the difference. Feel the difference.

5. Do send flowers. But not on the world's clock. Do it on your own clock. A random day with no meaning other than to say hello.

6. Do open the door for her—for God's sake! It's not needed every time, but occasionally, it is a sweet gesture.

7. Do respect boundaries. Stalking is *so L.A.* Let's keep that out of Dallas.

8. Do be open for love. Why do all this and have a closed heart? Take the leap of faith. Let it be worth it.

9. Do own something. Whether it's a home, an experience, or your story. Own it. You're much more desirable when you *own it.*

10. Do be at peace with yourself. Love yourself. You will attract so much more.

Don'ts

1. Don't call your ex names—bitch, c*nt, whore, etc . . . you get the picture. Just don't. Stop hating. Especially in front of your children.

2. Don't date your friend's ex. And, certainly, don't sleep with them.

3. Don't break the twenty-four-hour rule. If you have fucked someone in the morning, don't expect me to do the same with you twelve hours later. Especially, if you haven't showered. Gross.

4. Don't be a golddigger—at least not an obvious one. If you ask what he does for a living or what street he lives on in the first five minutes, he'll see right through you. You have a brain. Use it.

5. Don't tell her you love her a week after dating her. It's lust. Not love. Learn the difference.

6. Don't let your ex control you. Stop playing martyr. I prefer to date men who have a penis . . . not a pussy. That's my anatomical part. Not yours. Man up!

7. Don't talk out of both sides of your mouth. Say it and mean it. I'm done with men who are full of bullshit.

8. Don't leave me hanging via text. I still can't figure out the purpose behind starting a conversation and then ignoring answers. Have the decency to tell the other person you can't text, like in the old days. You just didn't hang up on a phone call. You said silly things like, "I have to run. I'll call you later. Bye." three letters. B.Y.E. It's not complicated and it tells the other person you are no longer able to engage. Seriously, it's the little things.

9. Don't pick me up in a red convertible Corvette. I'm not interested in your mid-life crisis. I'm only interested if you're past that. Your mind is your temple. Not your body. A little body fat is okay. I gave birth to four kids, I know what body fat is like.

10. Don't put me through your roller coaster. Been there, done that. The highs are great but the lows really suck. I'm not interested in that ride anymore, and I certainly wouldn't take my kids through it.

ABOVE ALL, DON'T BE FOR SALE. Have some integrity and remember, you're worth it and you'll figure it out. Re-program your software if it has viruses.

Permission to Orgasm . . .

Alright, this is a little different than the "Now you get to write about you" sections. Put that pencil down and get your ass in that bedroom, call your better half, do whatever it is you do—

and *scream!* If you don't have a better half right now, go solo. Even Charlotte went to town with her BOB on an episode of "Sex in the City" and eventually needed an intervention. We should all need one of those. Do it—*SCREAM!* It does a body good. You'll feel *so* much better.

Seriously . . . put this book down and go. Now!

Part 4

Numb in My Own Abyss

•

My 30s–40s

Chapter 15

Addicted to Addictions While Finding Comfort in Abuse

"Made a wrong turn, once or twice. Dug my way out,
blood and fire. Bad decisions? That's alright.
Welcome to my silly life."

—"F'ing Perfect," Pink—

s you've probably noticed, I allow my dear, sweet friend, Amy, the Amygdala, to make too many decisions for me. Because I'm always trying to understand and improve myself to take control of my emotionally charged decisions, I feel it's important to be open to non-traditional therapies. Hell, I've tried everything, so why not try something completely off the "normal" radar. A dear friend of mine recommended I seek the help of a spiritual healer, so I trekked forty-five minutes into the suburbs to go visit this spiritual healer. Yes, there's a first time for everything, and, yes, I said *spiritual.* This was not exactly my thing, but, at that point, I felt it couldn't hurt. Surely, I could dig deep into my subconscious and exorcise all those toxic demons that have been living the life of luxury inside the 10,000-square-foot home known as my head.

As the Healer swung the pendulum across the pages in her black, three-ring binder, which she flipped through many times, I sat there wondering *what the hell I'd gotten myself into now.* She was having a conversation with someone, but it wasn't me. I sat quietly and wondered if she was possibly talking to my dead grandfather.

I was too afraid to actually ask what the hell she was doing. Was this God, sending me His energy? Oh God, He knows *everything.* I remember thinking this couldn't be good. I feared He would divulge all my deepest secrets, then *would she* know? I looked at her face for any sign of this conversation she was obviously having and could tell nothing. She smiled at me and started talking.

"Let's start with your past life," she said. She explained I had been a monk who had been beheaded for abusing his wife. I was confused because I didn't think monks had wives. She then asked if I had any neck pain from the beheading I endured in my past life—with a straight face, no less! I became distracted, thinking how badly I wanted this woman in my poker group. *What?* Um, no my neck is just fine. Thanks, though. But now, whenever I do have back or neck pain, I'll be sure to blame the abusive monk I used to be in my past life because it certainly can't be from all the checking that goes on in ice hockey. Imagine telling the Doctor in the emergency room that my injury was sustained during a beheading in my past life as a Monk. He would immediately have me transferred to the psychiatric ward.

I begged her to stick with *this* life. I have enough to sort out in this life without having to deal with past lives. She seemed to be fine with my suggestion until she said, "Okay, then I won't tell you what God is telling me about your past life." Again, the pendulum swings, and she doesn't utter a word. I guess that monk *really* fucked up. While I stared at my phone and wondered how much longer my session was going to last, the Healer started talking again. Luckily, I had finally persuaded her to move on to *this* life. Thank God. I didn't think I could handle much more of this quackery.

Then she told me something I'd never thought of before. "You're addicted to guilt." *Finally.* She told me something

I had never been told before and had never crossed my mind. It made perfect sense that I was addicted to guilt. Her assessment could not have been more accurate. Why had I not already gleaned this from some of my self-help books? According to the spiritual healer, my guilt had been instilled in-utero. Perhaps a stretch on her part, but plausible. As my father was off getting laid by his secretary, who happens to be my current stepmother, my mother was transferring her damaged energy into my fetal self. That may sound a bit far-fetched, but I find it quite feasible. I can't blame all my bad decisions based on whatever energy was passed to me from her body during that painful time of her life. When you are a twenty-eight-year-old woman with three kids under the age of six and one more on the way, and you know *your* husband is fucking his secretary, that has to hurt. Considering that was nearly fifty years ago, one would think by now she'd moved on, but, to this day, my mother still hates him. I suffered that hate through childhood, my young adulthood, my wedding day, and even today—nearly five decades later. Good grief, she needs to move on—or should I be moving on? The jury is obviously still out on that one.

I've lived through a number of addictions in my life: sex, love, pills, alcohol, cigarettes, and, *now*, ladies and gentlemen, *guilt*. I have a guilt addiction. So many addictions, so little time. Some of them are fleeting and some rear their ugly heads once in a while. But, hey, I managed to quit the abusive behavior. This guilt addiction—thank you, oh spiritual guru—has stood the test of time. Let's count them down, shall we?

I feel guilty about my decision to end my marriage. I feel guilty about my affair. I feel guilty about the pain I caused to so many people, especially my children. I feel guilty about not being present for my children. I feel guilty every time I hit send, when I know I'm ranting. I feel guilty when I hurt the ones I love most. I feel guilty when I don't get everything done. I feel guilty every time I light a cigarette, every time I take another drink and then get behind the wheel when it might be deemed questionable. I feel guilty about having sex with the wrong men. I feel guilty about loving the wrong men. OH. MY. GOD. Does all this guilt ever end?

For far too long, I have been *consumed* with guilt. No wonder my mind won't ever shut down. It's as if the place in my head that holds all that shame and blame is a room, and the door has been forever locked. At least now I have an "excuse": I blame the monk.

How can I ever move forward with so much guilt consuming me? I've made some terrible decisions in my life, and I own them. I can't continue to torture myself over every poor decision I've ever made or will continue to make. Guilt has to have a shelf life. I need the guilt to have an expiration date so I can clear that room in my head and make it a place of peace, calm, and quiet. All of this corrosive real estate is taking up space in my mind. I know that all of this chaotic thinking stems from being abused as a child, and I shouldn't harbor an ounce of guilt, as I wasn't the one to blame, but I have felt guilt about my abuse that has morphed and manifested into so much more guilt in this lifetime. I know many of us feel this way. Imagine how many more people will be sexually assaulted by the time you finish reading this chapter.

So, I've made the decision, I'm going to KICK ADDICTION'S ASS and chip away at them, little by little. Goodbye, guilt. I am done with you. I've given up the pills, I control my drinking, and I am forging my way into a healthier and happier life. I still fight the fight. I'm better, but I'm still not where I want to be. When we first set goals, we aim so high, hoping for a better version of ourselves.

Part of fighting my guilt is to confront the reality of sexual abuse. Thanks to Harvey Weinstein and the #metoo movement, sexual harassment and sexual assault are in the news on a daily basis. Sexual abuse is one of our society's leading "silent crimes," but I will not stay silent. I'm not carrying this guilt anymore. I'm going to talk about it, and I'm going to do everything I can to get more people to talk about this horrid subject. Fuck you, pedophiles. You've messed with the wrong girl. The silence and rejection of the past has built a strong, intelligent woman who is unstoppable, and I know I'm not the only one.

The big question is: *How do we stop them?* Saving these children and protecting their purity and innocence from these abusers is something I fight for every day. Talking about this uncomfortable subject is the first step, but only the first one. Let's be realistic, nothing but tireless effort and taking action will do. I guarantee, some people will be afraid that they'll cause offense by encouraging others to act on any suspicions or concerns they may have. It's human nature to want to turn the other way with things we don't understand. Many will do nothing about it because of its taboo nature. Let's face it—as our society becomes more and more narcissistic, we tend to empathize less and less. Read: it's not affecting me, so why should I care? You should care and we should all care because of the far-reaching ramifications this heinous crime has on generations and all layers of society. There won't be any silence on my watch. Sorry, but with a crowd talking, it would be ideal if everyone would listen. Once enough voices are raised, it will be undeniable.

We will be heard, because we *need* to be heard. *We deserve to be heard.* We will protect our children from the men (and women) who help themselves. Until they get help, we must be LOUD, and must get even LOUDER. We were victimized, we suffered, and now we have a story to tell. In my heart, I hope my story will give someone the courage to speak out against an abuser. If you're reading this book and you've never had that uncomfortable conversation with your children because you never imagined it was a necessary conversation to have, now is the time to have it.

In case this is getting a bit too serious for you, here's a joke: "Why did the chicken cross the road?" Because the pedophile wasn't there. Not a laughing matter? *Make it one.* Laughter is where the healing starts. I've always been able to find humor in the most tragic of circumstances. I'm not sure if that's a gift or a curse. I've had to maintain a sense of humor through all my experiences, and I think this helps me share with others. My crazy-ass astrologer friend told me my chart reflected "a lot of emotional turmoil." *Are you kidding me?* The *good* news was that she said much of my emotional turmoil was meant to be, so I could help others and bring teaching to the world. Well, *thank you,* world. Here I am to teach.

I was born on Halloween and my friends say that certainly explains a lot. You throw in a birth year of 1969 and a name like Wanda, and there's my trifecta. 1969 was the year of the rooster. That also explains a lot about my cocky nature. I'm also a Scorpio, which makes me one dangerous, cocky woman. Wanda Elizabeth LaBounty, Born October 31, 1969. I was born on Halloween because my mother's obstetrician didn't want to miss the SMU football game, so he induced her a day early. One must find the irony in the fact that I was born on the one day of the year everyone gets to legitimately let the freak flag fly! C'mon, God, seriously?

One of the reasons I love Halloween is because it allows all of us to be someone we're not on a daily basis. For one day, we can be different without being judged. It lets your inner creative soul come out. It seems to me that most everyone I know is always someone they aren't. Very few of us are real. I mean *really real.* Most people won't allow themselves to be known on such an intimate level. No one is comfortable exposing one's innermost vulnerabilities. Why would we, anyway? Once you expose your weaknesses, sometimes others capitalize on them. Sometimes . . . sometimes, it's worth the risk to show your real you.

I've spent a lot of time and effort hiding the real me. The *real* victims here were my four children. I'm quite sure my children were short-changed for the first half of my forties. Sure, I was there *physically*, but I wasn't fully present *mentally or emotionally.* So, I'm fed up with myself but also fed up with my bad behavior. One can never be fully present when constantly numbing the mind and trying to escape from one's self. I have news for you. No matter where you go to escape, there you are. Just like when you're pregnant, you can't escape your body. When your heart is on the mend and you're digging deep, searching for something you've never had, you're still there. Stuck with yourself, your mind, and your own never-ending thoughts.

I spent the entire decade of my thirties changing diapers, just going from one kid to the next. My hands were certainly full during that time, but I was so busy taking care of my children, I forgot to live. I can barely remember those ten years, and, now, they are gone.

I had to ask myself if I was going to start *feeling* my life and start being present for my children, or if I was going to continue to numb myself. I was tired of self-medicating and just waiting for the day to end, just so the next one could come and go and repeat. I didn't want my forties to be a blur, just like my thirties had been. I had a hard time grasping how an *entire decade* could be a complete blur. I knew I hadn't drank my way through it. I had birthed four children and breastfed all of them. Okay, so I drank a little. When the breast milk is *green*, it's best *not* to drink it. Thus the saying, "pump and dump."

For years, I jockeyed for position. I welcomed the good, the bad, and the ugly. Yes, I was a mom that volunteered. I chaired many of my children's school fundraisers and collectively raised over a million dollars for the school. I made things happen. I was breastfeeding, changing diapers, and jockeying for position. I was trying to make a name for myself while still wanting to make a difference. I care, dammit, a great deal. I *really* do care. I wasn't sure if I was doing all this to avoid intimacy in my marriage, or if I really wanted to make a difference. The pressure was insurmountable. Here I was in my mid-thirties, vying to be the best Stepford wife in town.

Be perfect, Wanda. Smile, Wanda. Bake cookies, Wanda.

Fake it 'til you make it, Wanda.

Drink, Wanda.

In my mid-forties, there were so many difficult decisions to make. I knew I needed to dump the pills, the cigarettes, and other really bad day-to-day habits that kept me numb. I was so irritable. I had a very short fuse and was very short-tempered with my children at times. My choices were causing my behavior to be unfair to them. Instead of a mother, they got a monster that couldn't cope with day-to-day bullshit. Fuck that! I had to decide to toss it all out. I had to toss the mind-numbing pills and cigarettes. I said goodbye to the irritable, short-fused, asshole I had become. Let your children actually enjoy you and be *truly* present.

It wasn't the *stimulants* I was addicted to, it was the *stimulation*—which are two *very* different things. I know plenty of you are thinking, "Oh shit! I pop those pills, too, to numb my pain." After all, you can't go one day without seeing something in the media about America's opioid epidemic. The first step is to admit you have an issue, then you can mull it over for six or seven years and miss out on a lot of your life, just like I did. You'll miss a lot in your children's lives, too. It's your choice, and I'm not you, so I certainly can't make you do anything. I can't open your pill bottle and throw them down the toilet, but you can. Maybe, when you've had enough and you're fed up, you will do something about your problem, but maybe not. I implore you to at least try. Or better yet, I *challenge* you. I really do love a challenge.

Are you up for it? I was, and I did it. Just to be real, I'll still have a few drinks with my friends on occasion. Remember, I'm too vain to be a drunk, so there are no worries of alcohol consuming me. I'm just not going to behave badly around my children. Except for Halloween, when it's my birthday.

Ultimately, my family lost out, my children lost out, and my *soul* lost out. An apology won't bring my family back together, nor will it help heal the pain my ex-husband suffered at my horrific choices, so all that's left to change is my behavior. I fucked up and I own that. I have let guilt control my life for far too long, which forced me to make an enormous shift in my life. I have constantly told my children, "I don't want your apologies, I want a change in your behavior." It's high time I took my own advice. With the help of writing my blog, I slowly began learning how to turn this haphazard, anchorless, and now guiltless ship on a dime.

Chapter 16

Where Is My Anchor?

"I have run, I have crawled. I have scaled these city walls. But I still haven't found what I'm looking for."

—"I Still Haven't Found What I'm Looking For," U2—

Most people get their anchors from their parents. It's the parents' responsibility to provide their children with a sense of stability that helps provide their own anchor, but I didn't get that luxury. My parents divorced immediately after I was born because of my dad's affair—a story that happens to so many others every day. They had four children: two boys and two girls. They split the kids down the middle, much like you would a banana split you're sharing at Dairy Queen. The two girls go with Mom and the boys go with Dad and his wife and her three kids. If it sounds like *The Brandy Bunch*, it was really more like *Friday the 13th*: an emotional bloodbath.

My mother and Jim both had no issue tossing their children aside so they could be together. I fully understand that marriages fail, as mine certainly did. If you want to leave your spouse, though, don't leave your children. My ungrounded, anchorless childhood stemmed from the perfect storm: abandoned by my father, ignored by my mother and, sexually abused by my stepfather. To make that perfect storm, the true shit storm that it was, he was the only parental figure who showed me any sort of intimacy, whether it was appropriate or not. Simply put, that just fucks with your head. He made me give him oral sex, but then he would give me seventy-five cents to buy me an ice cream when the ice cream man pulled around the corner, blaring his music. Sadly, in those days, we should have been more worried about the ice cream man being a pedophile and not the man living inside your own home.

When people don't have an anchor, it's hard to have hope. When I went to my mother and told her I had been molested by her husband, SHE SHOULD HAVE DONE SOMETHING ABOUT IT. My mother acting on this information would have been providing me an anchor. Action gives your child hope that maybe they're not the ones doing something wrong or something to be ashamed of. Instead of providing support, though, I would go numb over some of the things that she'd go on to say in *his* defense. That Jesus Christ had forgiven him, and so should I. WRONG. Jesus could have forgiven him, who knows. The man is dead and has met his maker. I can only imagine how that conversation went. "Oh . . . it's you. We have a special place for you guys. It's a bit hot down there, but, luckily, you own a speedo. So, you'll be fine" (if you need to be reminded of the unfortunate visual—the pedophile mowing the lawn in his speedo with his gut hang-out out—go back to chapter seven).

A relationship with my mother was just not in the cards for me—at least not in this lifetime. Even after his funeral, I foolishly thought I could have a relationship with her. I thought once he had died, maybe she'd see that she hadn't been there for me and things would change. I don't know if that sounds utterly pathetic or just innocently hopeful. I thought that, finally, my mother would be the anchor in my life she was always meant to be. Truth be told, I have no respect for my mother. It took me a really long time to accept this. Now, I've come to realize we truly have *nothing in common*. She's not athletic. She doesn't have a great sense of humor. She's narrow-minded in her thinking. There's nothing even particularly interesting about her: she's not well-read and she's not well-traveled. *Nothing.* Plus, I've always hated the way she dresses. Her sisters, however, are both great mothers. Mind you, all three women grew up without a mother; I never understood how they all turned out so differently and why I couldn't have had one of her sisters as my mother. Maybe I'll be more fortunate in my next life. I've tried to forgive my mother. They say forgiveness isn't to benefit the person who committed the foul, but it will benefit you. You forgive for your own sanity. Finally, I summoned the courage to forgive her for being a weak woman. But, as hard as I've tried, I just don't have it in me to forgive her for staying with the man who caused me so much pain.

My real father is even more impossible to forgive. I never really had the chance to get to know him, probably because my mother blamed him for so much. The clock is ticking on our ability to have any sort of relationship. He has always been too busy raising his wife's kids to be bothered to spend any quality time with me. Sure, I would see him during the holidays and in the summer—but he couldn't be bothered to show up to my high school graduation. His wife's boys were graduating college at the same time. Priorities, I suppose. I'm just grateful he didn't sexually abuse me, too. Pedophilia wasn't his thing. He had other weaknesses. His biggest weakness was his inability to put his children first, and he knows it. He admitted this to me one cold and rainy Mother's Day at an IHOP in Garland, one of Dallas' suburbs. He even asked how he could make it up to me, and I told him it would be great if he would come by the following week for my daughter's 13th birthday. Do you think he showed up? That's a big fat NOPE. No phone call. No text. Nothing. Absolutely ZERO communication. Thanks, Dad, for bringing up all the same nightmarish childhood emotions I've managed to suppress. Sometimes having hope is so depressing.

Even though my father could never be my anchor, I thought he might at least be present in my children's lives. I so desperately wanted my son to have a relationship with his grandfather. I tried when my oldest was young, but after a few disappointing family events, I stopped trying. As if it wasn't bad enough that he rejected me, it hurt considerably more when he rejected my son. Thank God for Facebook! I get the pleasure of seeing my father being a doting grandfather. Just not to my children. The SOB was always at his wife's kids' and grandkids' events and not mine. God, that sucks. I've stopped trying to forge any relationship between him and my kids.

My parents should have been my anchor. Since that was never possible, though, where is my anchor? Ships come with them, I know. I always seek my anchor in the form of another person. I feel that if I don't hold onto another person—in the form of a man that's a love interest—I may float away. Where is my internal anchor, though? I've found it difficult to let go of yet another man in my life even when this one said he didn't want me. ALL of my friends used to tell me I deserved better; even he would tell me I deserved better, but I was stubborn and didn't want to listen. I was really just afraid of being alone. I was afraid of "floating": of being out there with no man to anchor me because I couldn't anchor myself. God, that is so fucking pathetic! I wish I could just push a button and uncoil my own anchor. I need to figure out a way to build that internal anchor for myself.

I'm working on the whole "love" and "relationship" anchor with men. With one man in particular, I've thrown the anchor overboard and lifted it so many times, I have serious biceps. But that is what life is about. As long as I know in my heart that my children are safe and the man in my life is not hurting them, the onus is on me for my heart. My current partner is a great father to his kids and is good to my kids. This is one aspect I would never negotiate in romantic relationships, but I know I am still a work in progress when it comes to matters of the heart. Sometimes, I feel the man I am with is my anchor, and, at other times, I feel like he's sinking me like the Titanic.

Despite my own instability and inability to feel anchored, I have learned one important lesson: I have to be my children's anchor. I've made sure they won't be "anchorless." It's a battle I wage every single day. Once the pedophile stated that my eight-month-old son's haircut was "sexy," I was done. Gone. Goodbye, fucker. His careless statement hit me so hard that the numbness finally wore off. I pulled up that anchor and this ship sailed. As the captain, I would protect my kids to the inth degree. For that matter, we should also become our friends' anchors, as well. I am a *great* friend to my friends. Loyal, dedicated, and would do just about anything for them. I am their anchor, and, in many ways, they are mine.

Fortunately, when I rise in the morning and put my head down to sleep at night, I *know*, in my very soul, I am my children's anchor and they are mine. They keep me grounded, focused, and very, *very* busy. Four kids will do that, but they know they can rely on me no matter what. I am there for them, 24/7. All I could depend on from my parents was having them disappoint me. Their religious devotion didn't give me any sort of anchor, either. Because my religious anchor was so full of hypocrisy, it had no use. Faith and religion often anchor those with so little in life—but not me.

Some things just need to start at a young age. Skating is one; feeling the unconditional love of your parents is another because that is where your anchor originates. It's like hockey. I've been playing hockey now since my early thirties. I can skate, I can score, and I know how to play the game, but the fact is, I will never be a great skater, simply because I didn't learn to skate as a child. But my personality is such that I will always strive to be a good person, a good parent, and a good friend, and just maybe, a decent skater. Anchors away!

Chapter 17

My Post Prepubescent, Post Natal, Pre-Menopausal Testosterone-Induced Zit

"Hold onto 16 as long as you can. Changes come around real soon making us women and men."

—"Jack and Diane," John Cougar—

Nothing like a college reunion to make you realize you aren't in college anymore. No way was I going to peak before my time. But still, forty-five and I still get pimples. Really? I somehow escaped getting those in high school and college. Occasionally, one would pop up on my face in my teens. At which point, my friends had no problem announcing to everyone that I had a zit. I can't complain. Nothing, and I mean nothing, is normal about me. When one is forced to give their first GCBJ (Good Christian Blow Job) at eight, they are destined for a life that will never be normal. So, I go with it. I go with the flow. Or at least try most days. Some days, I just want to be normal, but that's probably not in the cards for me. What does that mean, anyway?

So, I went to my college reunion, and one of my sorority sisters screams "OMGaaaaaaad . . . you look exactly the same . . ."

God, I hope not. Heard that about fifty times that weekend at my twenty-plus year college reunion. I've given birth to 4 humans who sucked everything out of me: there's no fucking way I look the same! I've gone through a divorce. I've hit bottom more than once. I wear the "scar" let letter across my chest and forehead. I may have colored the greys but they manage to pop up every friggin' month, a reminder to touch up my roots, get that face cream to hide the lines (do they really work?), and try some spiritual awakening to hide the emotional scars. "Look the same?" Doubtful.

As my zit and I walked into this reunion, it became so clear that, sadly, people are so fucking fake, even years later. I see them coming a mile away. Someone I know said, "If only we could hold up people in the light like we do hundred dollar bills to see if they are real or not!" Whereas I show scars accumulated, they show "material things" accumulated over the past twenty-plus years. Awesome. Call me when you're ready to have a real conversation. Until then, my A.D.D. has set in. Again. I have no interest in your self-perceived portrait of success. Believe me, I see right through you. These are women who are six months older and one grade ahead of me in college and STILL acting like it means something twenty years later. Give me a break. One of them told me I was still so young and had so much to learn. Um, really? GIRL, you couldn't even keep up with me if you sprinted the marathon one-hundred times over. She was so patronizing.

But some were real, and that I admire. A few managed to open up to the addictions people close to them were suffering. I fully appreciated that. Makes me not feel so alone out there. However, it was always about somebody else. Not theirs. I guess it's so much easier to talk about other people's issues versus your own. For the love of God, can anyone open up and really be honest about their lives? No need to discuss my life. Apparently, they had already read my blog. After all, I don't hold back on anything. I was able to stay with my pledge sisters, and we had a blast, the highlight of this reunion.

What shocked me the most was how fanatical everyone still was about the football games. I know a lot of people are fans of college football. Maybe it takes them back to a time in their life before reality set in? Those four years of college are so close to reality, yet so far removed from it. I guess watching college football keeps people young. Or stunts them. I'm not exactly a football fanatic (note, "fan" is short for "fanatic"), but I have a true love and appreciation for the game. Total Dallas Cowboys fan as a kid, by the way.

But I have four kids and watch them play sports every single weekend. I don't have time to watch college football. As my friend Alison puts it, "If my son isn't playing, I'm not watching. I spend all my weekends sitting in the stands, watching him." Why the hell are we here watching a football team of *nobody* we know just because we went to college there twenty years ago? I'm pretty sure there are other events going on in life besides college football.

One quarter and we are done. We leave the stadium and trek across campus to our college bar, appropriately named Dirtbags. "A part of growing up": that's their slogan. Indeed, it was a HUGE part of my growth during my stint in college. Though I may be decades older, walking in made me feel like I was twenty-one again. The same bartender was there twenty-five years later. Wow! I'm speechless. They still ring the bell whenever someone leaves a generous tip. Rich college kids LOVE to be generous with their parents' money, but not me. I didn't have that luxury. We stand around waiting for a table in "our" bar—mixed with overly inebriated, half-dressed college kids and my peers trying to relive their youth, while documenting every step of the way on Facebook. Part of me is nostalgic, but the other part doesn't want to touch *anything*—I didn't remember this place being so sticky. Yuck. Wow, I really have grown up. It was probably this gross in college, and I didn't even care, but now I want to break out the bleach and wipe everything and everyone down.

So how is it that we all look "the same" to our friends from long ago, but all the current college students look so damn young? And, what's with these outfits? Tube tops were every-where I looked and shorts up the ass. Sure, I could put that outfit on and make a complete ass of myself—that I'm capa-ble of! But who really wants to see my stretch marks from my four children and my saggy, falling breasts? You know the ones. Apparently, my children are stronger than gravity. They had the power to suck everything out of them and used such force that dragged them down to my knees. Here I was, saggy breasts and all, surrounded by college kids who don't have a care in the world but what's currently around them. Party, drink, find a girl, find a guy, take some classes, or, better yet, sleep through them, but, most importantly, have a good time. I remember those days.

It was a very surreal experience. I also learned how brave some of my sisters have been over the years and what they've gone through. We talked (and drank) a lot, and their stories truly had an impact on me. Like me, some of them had been through a divorce and were facing the same issues I was, like raising children as a single parent. Almost all of them had known my story and weren't that shocked to see my story shared with others on the internet through my blog. None of them were shocked by my bluntness. I guess some things never change.

Though I loved seeing my sisters and traipsing through old times at the bar, I've come to realize that I have lived an entire life since college. My children, alone, keep me busy. Having four kids who have played four sports each year over the past fifteen years, means I have been to A LOT of games. Plus, I have my own games to play, and I still travel for my own tournaments that I still get to enjoy.

I've come to the realization that, although I may have been a bit wild in my thirties and forties, the reunion made it clear that I have grown up. I am a good mother to my children and responsible enough to ensure they are growing up in the best way possible. My son will be starting college in a year. God help me then. All I can do is make sure he's responsible and stalk him (I love you so much sometimes, social media).

Thank you to my Alpha Phi sorority sisters, for allowing me to go back in time with you. I still love you guys. But I am very grateful for the life I have today. 3 days of that time travel, and I'm slapped in the face with a reality check. Aka, a hangover. Can't sit around all day drinking anymore. I have to get to class. I mean . . . life.

This Section's All Yours
Confronting Addictions, Planting Anchors

1. What are your addictions?

2. If you're honest with yourself, would you say there's some comfort in being addicted to your addictions?

3. In what ways do you numb the pain? How is it serving you?

4. Who, or what, is your anchor? How did you realize that, you had this anchor in your life?

5. Are you the anchor for anyone else?

6. Compare yourself now to when you were twenty-one. How have you "grown up?" On the other side of this question: are there ways that your growth has been stunted?

Part 5

Ending the Numbness
Finally Feeling the Pain

•

My 40s—Now

Chapter 18

Nomadic No More

"But today the way I play the game is not the same, no way. Think I'm gonna get myself happy."

—"Freedom," George Michael—

inally, I can breathe. It's been a few years since my divorce, but those first years were anything but an easy transition. I can't remember when I was that challenged. I felt like a nomad then, but I ultimately grew weary of moving—of feeling like I didn't have a real home. I was renting, packing, unpacking, renting again, and packing again. When does it stop? Condos, rental houses, duplexes—on and on and on. I needed a home for my children and me. I needed roots. I finally made the decision to move out of this exorbitantly overpriced neighborhood that was my home for nearly twenty years.

Being married for almost seventeen years was already more stability than I was ever accustomed to as a kid. Don't forget, my mother was married four times by the time I was seven, and we moved more times than I can remember. My siblings and I went to a total of about ten elementary schools. Oddly enough, I do remember the four different elementary schools I went to. I felt like a gypsy growing up. Here, there, and everywhere. No stability in my home nor my school. My ability to make friends and play sports was the only thing that grounded my gypsy soul. The family life I had created in my late twenties gave me the sense of normalcy that I never had growing up. Creating consistency, normalcy, and ROOTS for my children was one of my most important tasks. I would be damned if my children had to experience any of my gypsy upbringing.

But divorce would have other plans, especially with an angry, hurt man on my hands. It wasn't normal for us to fight, but I should have known that cheating on him would strip him to his very core. I get it. What I wanted to make sure, above all, was that my kids wouldn't feel the backlash of my horrid mistakes in any way. They would feel some, for sure, but I would do my utmost to keep them as stable as possible, even though I was a complete mess inside. Fake it till you make it. It was time to make a decision about where my kids and I would live. Though I have a wild streak, and it may stick with me for the rest of my life, I am uber conservative as a mother. As much craziness as I have, I'm doing my damnedest to shield them from it. My babies know me well enough at this stage, especially my oldest one, to be certain that I always have their best interests at heart. My oldest son knows that I'm a fighter, and, no matter what, he and his siblings are safe and loved.

They also know they better work damn hard. I may be wild as a woman and conservative as a mother, but, above all, I have a work ethic that is anything but subpar. Even though my kids all have different potentials, I want to be sure that all have a similar work ethic. I have to, have to, have to make sure they know to keep their word, be kind and compassionate to others, refrain from bullying (it won't get you anything), and try to make a difference. And do their homework, dammit. No matter how many times I had to uproot my children during this phase of post-apocalyptic divorce, they had consistency on a daily basis, based purely on the fact that their mother and father loved them.

So, I ventured across Central Expressway, the major highway separating the ultra-rich from the not so ultra-rich (or, as I like to say, "the comfortable"). I bought a piece of land on the "other side of the tracks" and moved east. Twenty years was long enough in this town. Don't get me wrong—I'm a mere three blocks from my ex-husband. I'm quite sure my children can make the trek across all the rough "terrain"—the bridge (with a pedestrian walkway) over the highway. It may as well be the other side of the world according to my kids. "Mom, this is so far . . . " Really? Three blocks? I'm sure we've all heard the story from our parents, who had to trek 20 miles in the snow, uphill both ways, every day with old shoes. Blah, Blah, Blah. It's Texas, people, there's practically no snow here! Have you checked the Texas Almanac for snowfall for the past one-hundred years in Houston, where my mother grew up? Umm . . . not near as deep as my mother portrayed the snow to be.

I'm building a house on this beautiful piece of land, and I'm excited, as I love the building process. I love to turn ideas into reality. More importantly, I'm finally getting roots. So hard to lay roots in a town that you never felt like you belonged to. After all these years raising my children here, I still feel like a fish out of water. Perhaps, that's why I always felt like a gypsy. Hmmm . . . I can only wonder. You can take the gypsy out of the lower-middle class, but you can't take the gypsy out of the girl. As I venture on my own with my children in tow, I wonder, "Can the house keep me rooted or will I constantly be longing for something else?" Houses are nothing but a bunch of lumber, concrete, and maybe a few cute light fixtures. It's up to me to make it a home, and to do so without a partner in life. I have to ask myself if I'm up for this. Is my anxiety really gone or not, as I am forever searching for the ever-elusive peace and roots?

I've made the decision to be fiscally conservative, all the while leaving my children and ex-husband the option to stay close to each other. I have no desire to be cash-poor, and building a house gives the kids and me exactly what we want but without the ultra-rich address. Oh well, we can't have everything, can we? I'm happy with my decision, and that's the best part. I'm thrilled to be living in some semblance of diversity. Not much diversity in the school district my children attend. There's no shortage of blond haired, blue-eyed kids in this town. Including my four. Of course, I'm being my usual sardonic self.

Well, I'm still "in town," but, truth be told, I would rather be on the water. I love the water, but it's just not in the cards right now. I'm OKAY, though. I designed and built this beautiful house myself. As I look around, I see me and my children everywhere. Whereas, I'm so damn exhausted from cracking the whip in a very condensed amount of time, I'm so damn proud of what I built. Building it was the easy part. Decorating is a beast of its own. So not my thing. Thank God for friends with an eye for decorating. That's a talent that skipped my genes.

With lots of elbow room, my children and I are comfortable at our new home. The house is very lively with my mini-me's and their friends running around every day. There's never a shortage of something to do, somewhere to go, and someone to see. As an unpaid Uber driver, I spend hours on the road shuffling them to all of their events. Nobody said being a single parent was easy. Luckily, my ex is only a few blocks away and almost always available to help, even though one of us inevitably has to draw the short straw to run Robert all over the map for club hockey. I'm quite sure club sports weren't designed to suit single parents. Anyone who has done this knows exactly what I'm talking about. All of my children have participated in club sports at one point or another. Thank God for a good ex-husband and carpools.

I'm exhausted with three different schools, four children, homework, sports, tutors, an endless amount of after school snacks, two teenagers with one on the way in and another on the way out, and a food budget through the roof. The list goes on and on. And yet, with all of this craziness called life, I have rooted my children and me. Considering what I had to work with growing up, I'm a proud woman. And a tired mom.

Chapter 19

You Are a Badass

**"I'm a bitch, I'm a lover, I'm a child, I'm a mother,
I'm a sinner, I'm a saint."**

—"Bitch," Meredith Brooks—

It felt good to have solid roots in my new home, even though I still keep my bedroom door closed at night. I guess some fears are so deeply rooted in me and will never go away, but I can always find a way to adjust. Other than that, I'm on solid ground for the first time since my divorce. This year, since I'm finally in a home I'm proud to call mine, we decided to have Christmas at my house rather than Richard's. For ten years, we have had a family tradition: we go see Santa Claus at the downtown Neimans on Christmas Eve, followed by a bottomless meal at The Palm restaurant in Dallas' West End. I'm proud of my ex-husband. He had every reason to be bitter, but he chose, then, and he still chooses, now, our children over his feelings. Christmas has always been about the kids, and just because we live in two different homes, doesn't mean we aren't still a family. We both choose to put our children above our feelings, and I know they are better off with us getting along in two homes rather than being miserable together in one.

As with any Christmas, I never expect much. After many years of disappointment from my parents, it's simply second-nature for me to expect nothing. However, that year I received a gift from my oldest, my son that shook me to my very emotional core. I certainly wasn't expecting it. It was a little yellow book, *You are a Badass*. Of all the books he could have given me, he gave me this one. I could not be more shocked. What sixteen-year-old gives that to his mother? I certainly never thought of my mother as a "badass." I thought of my mother as more of a pathetic weak-ass. I'm sure he saw the title and thought, "Yep, my mom is a badass." I still wonder if this is what he thinks of me.

Truth be told, I did build my house in ninety days and made a million decisions with the clock ticking. I guess that technically makes me a "badass." But, I'm the farthest thing from a "badass," when it comes to love and relationships. I couldn't be more of a failure in that area of my life. The book's premise is to change the self-sabotaging beliefs and behaviors that stop you from getting what you want. He couldn't have been more dead-on with this gift. Did he know that's what he was getting for me? Can a sixteen-year-old boy be that astute? Mine certainly can be, as he's my independent thinker. Most kids want nuggets and fries at the age of three. Not this kid. He wanted sushi, fresh vegetables, and fruit. What a mature palate—albeit expensive as hell. He loves my cooking, but isn't shy about saying, "Mom, not the best meal you've prepared." So, when I look down at my Christmas gift and see a self-help book from my teenager, I was speechless. My son, Richard, is truly an anomaly. What an incredible gift—this book with so much meaning. This is what he thinks of me. I'm a "badass" that needs some self-love. I'll take that.

Before this year, my children had never actually purchased a gift for me. All I've ever wanted was a handwritten card. For every card they create, I know there is unconditional love.

Other than that, the gift of time with them is what I really want. Material things have little purpose to me. I have a saying: "Toys are more fun—if you share them." I do have some really nice things that I indulge myself with on occasion, but my kids want material THINGS. They are under a lot of peer pressure, and I totally get that. I won't feed into it much, but I understand it. They want things they see everyone else has. Like those damn hover boards, for instance. As much as I tell them those things will only satisfy you for about five minutes, they just don't get it. While my girls were in middle school, I was fighting a losing battle in this town where the money seems to grow on trees. They like to shop, but I don't. I reluctantly gave them my credit card this year and sent them on their mission to buy gifts for me and their dad. Lizzie had already used the money she earned making good grades to buy her sister and brothers their gifts. Yep. She works her ass off all semester to make straight A's, and then uses her cash to buy her siblings' gifts. That's a proud parenting moment that makes up for some of those not so proud parenting moments.

Off they go on their mission to buy me something. Sweet. Not necessary but thoughtful, nonetheless. The girls bought me a coffee mug with a moose on it from Keystone. Perfect. I drink coffee every day, so, now, as I sip my coffee, my thoughts can trail off to our family skiing vacation in Keystone. That gift meant a lot because the trip meant a lot. I love to take a quick getaway to the slopes, to refresh my spirit and take my kids with me. Experiences (especially in the snow) are far better than ANY material "thing." My nine-year-old son is already better than me at skiing. He is my fearless leader down the hill on those slippery slopes. "Follow me, Mom." Words I'm not used to hearing. Love that! It was just two years ago that I had to hold him between by legs, while he was on his skis, and haul him down the mountain. ALL THE WAY down the mountain! Talk about an exhausting experience! I've taught all of my kids how to play sports, but teaching them how to ski? I need professional help for this. I bought him a private lesson from an incredible instructor, and my boy is teaching me how to be a better skier! Best $400 I ever spent. Talk about a return on your investment! There are few things I enjoy more than skiing with my little guy. Now, I can remember all of that from a coffee mug. It's the little things that tell me I've done something right.

I have no recollection of the gifts I received from my father growing up, and very few items from my mom and step-pedo-philiac (not actually a word in the dictionary, yet). I do remember my dad buying us a George Foreman grill when I was older, but only because he bought one for everyone else. Meaningless. I remember chotchke items he would bring from conventions, too. Like candy with a label on it: "For our services, think of us in the future." Is that supposed to having meaning? Maybe. Well, at least he thought about us for a whole thirty seconds. Thanks, Dad. Don't even get me started about my mother.

My son, though, has given me more than just the book as a present. He's given me the gift of being an independent, driven, and loving son—all that any mother wants. The morning after Christmas Day, before the sun has even risen, I had to drive sixteen-year-old, Richard, to the airport. He's off to Camp Pendleton for a nine-day mini boot camp for his naval sea cadet program in San Diego. I had zero to do with this decision. He did it all. Even cut his hair to a *number one* buzz cut. His hair. I loved his hair longer. But, it's gone now. It'll grow back, right? Sure, I had to sign the necessary paperwork and write a check to pay for the experience. But he did everything else. He purchased all the necessary supplies. Packed his own bag. I don't even know what's in his government issued green bag. You've seen those bags—all the Navy guys have them! For the first time in his life, I had zero contact with him for the entire nine days. It's not like camp, where they post pics online, so you can see how much fun your kid is having at sleep away camp. Nope. Nothing. In the dark. For nine whole days. This is his adventure. His father and I are just underwriting it.

In my book, my son is the badass. You go get'em, Rich. This badass mom couldn't be prouder of her badass son! For all the pathetic Christmases I had as a kid, you make up for them by just being your badass self. Thank you for reminding me of that.

The greatest gift I can ever give my children is their father and I still being in each other's lives. Many more Christmases will come and go, and we will be together. Even as my children vie for more material gifts, because getting older simply does that, they will always have the love and care of their parents. THAT is the most important gift I can give myself and them. The rest, well, it's just immaterial.

While my oldest son has taught me how to recognize my badass-ness, my oldest daughter has taught me how to say "I love myself." Lizzie loves to draw. She can sit in her room for hours, drawing and creating. The other day I saw one of her drawings. All it said was, "I love myself." Wow! Job well done, Wanda and Richard! Confidence and self-esteem: those are some of the most important gifts we can give our children. On top of that, it's a gift to love yourself. I've never written that down—"I love myself." So, I did. It's working—sometimes I actually even feel that way. I wish I believed it more. If it takes time for our children to learn their ABC's and mathematics, perhaps it will take me a while to learn how to love myself.

I know, in my heart, if I keep writing it down, keep saying it to myself, I will eventually be really good at it. Repetition, repetition, repetition, gets us closer to where we want to be. Not striving for perfection, but I will strive to get to a better, healthier, and more balanced place. Because I'm worth it. Damn, Loreal, that commercial really sunk in. We should all love ourselves. I'm actually starting to believe this. "I love me, I'm worth it, I'm strong, and I'm beautiful." I keep saying these words to myself, and they are finally really starting to sink in. Out with the old beliefs, in with the new. I've been practicing my self-love, my affirmations, and I'm getting a new love. I'm moving on to a better love. Me, myself, and I. About time. I'm saying it, repeating it, and I want to believe it. It's better to keep practicing than for your mind to continually beat itself up. Good for me.

Me. Breathing, chanting, writing. Of course, this is hurting me. I have to work double time with myself at this point. I want to raise my children with self-esteem. I want them to grow up believing they can be anything they want to be. Internally and externally. Chant, Wanda, believe in yourself. I'm breathing, thanks to my children.

I can't get over how different my kids' relationships are with me, compared to my own relationship with my mother. They are teaching me how to see myself in a positive light. When I look for a Mother's Day card for my mother, I search for a card that says, "Happy Mother's Day . . . thank you for not drowning me at birth!" Hallmark doesn't make those cards, though . . . or at least, I couldn't find one. On that note, where is the Father's Day card that says, "Happy Father's Day, hope you're enjoying your new family!" Love, your daughter Wanda." Can't find that one either. So, instead, I go with a generic, "Happy Mother's Day, from your Favorite Daughter." I was being a bit of a smart ass, too. I would eventually get to the point where I would just order flowers for my mother. Meaningless and effortless. But on Mother's Day, I'm really not feeling it. I don't want to look for a card or send her anything. I'm done. When my friends tell me, "Get away from her, Wanda, it's toxic," you know it's serious. But I go back and forth with my emotions, confused over whether I should be the dutiful daughter or abused daughter. I don't want to be angry anymore.

I've gone as deep and dark as I want to go. I've cried my last tear. No longer will any undeserving person—mother, father, or man—be given my love. I would rather have an imperfect love than a perfect deception. For all of you out there who haven't had the love you deserve, I'm telling you to chant: *I DESERVE LOVE. I AM WORTH IT.*

There is no such thing as a perfect love. I've gained some solace, knowing I am working on myself, and I've given up chasing after my father. I've tried to love him, but, quite frankly, he isn't worthy of it. He left over forty-eight years ago, and, clearly, has no intention of coming back. Oh well. His loss. I'm done giving and giving and giving. If you don't want me or love me, then so be it. I can no longer sit here and cry over a father who never was. It's simply not healthy. No longer will I go for men like my father. No longer will I be second fiddle.

I've had several men carry me through their emotional cycles, just like my father did. When men are selfish, it hits all of my internal and emotional triggers, but I tried to hang in there. On again, off again. Over and over. It was like the emotional abuse I had to endure from my father, in some ways. Now, though I have my armor—an inner belief system—I won't ever take crumbs from a man again. When I realize I'm no longer a priority and am made to feel neglected, I'm out the door. I have no issue wiping my hands clean of an unhealthy relationship.

The battle in my head is real. Do you know how many thoughts can fit into a black hole. An infinite amount. And therein lies my challenge. Healing and wanting. Needing something that I know I can't have right now. Yet, I know I am working hard on myself and getting my self-esteem in check. I'm a good mother, check! I'm a good woman, check! I'm great at business, check! I excel in sports, check! I have a big heart, check! I'm a good coach, check! I'm an excellent friend and make a difference in people's lives, BIG check! I'm a good Christian, oops, can't check that one off yet. I'm a good human being, check! Yes, we will go with that one.

This amazing woman is learning to love herself and getting rid of all the toxicity in her life. It's damaging and benefits no one. It's not an easy road, but, then, who wants the easy way out of anything? I was made to have more challenges than most, I suppose. So I can help others. Either way, good or bad, hard or easy, I'm on a path. Blessed to have good children, friends, and, especially, myself.

Hello, Wanda. Look forward to getting to know you. And love you. Your turn. Say that to yourself. Trust me, it works.

Chapter 20

Finding Clarity in Unconsciousness

"This one's for the girls. Yeah, we're all the same inside, from one to ninety-nine."

—"This One's for the Girls," Martina McBride—

I am lucky to have friends and family who are an important part of my life and share in it. I am a lucky woman, indeed. I have never been more sure of this than after my early morning car accident I had in the fall of 2015. Someone, something, or some higher power was definitely watching over me. Choices we make every day can affect us: the big, little, impulsive, and even the subconscious choices. There are so many choices we make each day, whether we make them consciously or simply on autopilot. We make them, and, with each choice, there are always consequences. All of our actions have a consequence, whether intended or not—even a car accident. Obviously, I did not make the choice to get into an accident. Because of the accident, I realized just how many people I had around me who cared and supported me. I was able to find clarity in that unconscious moment.

The night before the accident, I woke up in the middle of the night with horrific, incredibly painful stomach cramps. The pain was unbearable. I was powerless while this twenty-four-hour virus completely took control of my body and mind. I sat there anticipating a mass exodus of *everything* in my body. I was weak, dehydrated, and doubled over in writhing pain. I felt like I was about to give birth, as the contractions were so intense, except I wasn't pregnant. Of course, I couldn't sleep. Never mind my pain or exhaustion, as I am a mother and had to take my seventh-grade daughter to volleyball before the crack of dawn. I had asked my son to take her for me, but he complained he was too tired to get up, and I was already too spent to argue. Doubled over in pain, I had no other choice but to get in the car. Kids. Parenting. Life. It's what you do. Sick or not. We march on.

This was not the day to act like I could do it all, because I couldn't. As I dropped my daughter off at school, the pains kept coming. I was still in my car but had to throw up and felt another bout of diarrhea coming on. My body was in a tailspin. All I wanted to do was get back home, so I took the fastest route. As the nausea kicked in, I made a last minute, split-second decision to *not* get on the highway. I have no idea why, but, in that moment, I chose to veer right instead of left. This turned out to be a life-changing decision for me. As I stayed on the frontage road, all I wanted to do was throw up. I was dizzy and light-headed and dehydrated from the previous night's date with my toilet. In an instant, I blacked out, while driving thirty-some-odd miles per hour on the front road at six o'clock in the morning.

A few minutes later, I came to. I was so confused that I actually thought I was in my own driveway for a moment but couldn't decide how I'd gotten there because the last thing I remembered was being on the frontage road. I was a mess, my head was groggy, and I had no idea where I was or how I'd gotten there. I unfastened my seatbelt and thanked God I was wearing one. When I got out of my car, I saw that I had hit some sort of a wall or building. I threw up and had diarrhea again. All on the side of the road. I'm in my pajamas, with no bra on, no panties on, and no shoes. I was a fucking mess.

After seeing my car, I couldn't believe I had simply walked away unscathed. Well, except for my own viral waste running down my legs. Someone was definitely watching over me.

No one was on the front road at the time, so there were no witness, and, more importantly, no victims. I hadn't taken either of my usual routes and had chosen not to get on the highway. The neighborhood route would've been full of early morning joggers, and the highway would've been full of early morning commuters. I would have either killed me or someone else had I taken either route. Due to my severed belief system and lack of faith, I'll never understand why I chose this less traveled option. Someone, or something, though, was watching over me.

Additionally—and here is where I am really lucky—I had someone to take care of me after the fact. When I finally realized I'd totaled my car, I called my ex-husband. Richard and I are more than just the parents of our four children, we are still family. I take full ownership of being the catalyst for our divorce, but just because we had a failed marriage doesn't mean we can't have a successful divorce. Richard quickly came and took care of me. As grateful as I remain that I chose him to be the father of my children, I am truly more grateful he is still in my life, to help me constantly pick up the pieces. He still is, and will always be, my family, and he still cares about me, even after all the damage I caused. Although we weren't meant to be as a couple, we were meant to be as a family. That is part of my clarity.

Richard pieced together the accident based on tire marks and car paint on the median. He said I had swerved, hit, and ricocheted—and fucking survived what clearly could have been tragedy. I missed the telephone pole by a mere twelve inches. Clearly, I am not meant to die anytime soon, whether it's by my own choice or someone else's. I am meant to believe and have faith that someone or something is watching over me. I am meant to be here for my children, so I can hug them harder each night, love them more, and show them how to survive and thrive in life. I am meant to make a difference in my life and the lives of others. Not only am I meant to be here, but I am meant to be here fully.

As I look back on this accident and the flood of support afterwards, I realize I am truly in a much better place. It was a cathartic moment in my life that would turn everything around. Have you had one of those? It made me realize that I have found some stability, and I need to embrace this stability, find my inner peace, adjust my pace, and calm the fuck down. I've done nothing but uproot my own life and my children's, so now it's hard to accept the feeling of being rooted. But, I've realized that it's now up to me to make the decisions that will affect not only myself, but the family I love and adore.

Somehow, some way, in this scary moment in my life, I created a stronger and more stable person within myself. Stability, of course, doesn't mean my mind has made a complete 180 from its normal, hectic state. Instead, it means finding a way to work with my mind.

My brain is in constant motion, so it's hard to sit, sleep, and it's challenging to be quiet, even for an hour for yoga. It's hard for me to sit still for a three-hour dinner, having the same monotonous conversation with the *same* people about the *same* things. I need action, interaction, and constant stimulation. It's exhausting. I probably took pills just to turn my mind off. I didn't ask for this hand I was dealt: this constant need for stimulation was dealt to me by my molester. He determined my fate. My shrink told me, "When young children get this kind of stimulation at such a young age, their brain is forever altered. They should never receive this much stimulation at such a young age." BAM! Explains a lot. Too much stimulation at such a young age is NOT healthy. It sets the tone for a lifetime of incessant need for more, more, and more.

This constant need is confusing because what I really want most of all is peace. Sure, I can hop a plane to a fabulous beach and leave my worries behind, but what happens when I come back? They're waiting for me when I return. No matter where I go, there they are. The constant stimulation my brain requires is usually in the form of negative thoughts. Even when my life has some semblance of peace, I tend to sabotage it. I just want a vacation from myself, my head, my thoughts, my demons. I'm running a million miles an hour inside my head, and I just can't stop.

There are times when it's not so crowded or negatively noisy in my head. Like when I'm playing hockey or in work mode and in full concentration. It's all the other times that I can't seem to stop my brain from feeling, as though it's going to blow up. Sometimes, I think the luxury of an unconditional love from the one person who is supposed to love me—my mother—would help calm my mind. I don't have that luxury, because, for me, that mother doesn't exist. My fantasy of her actually holding my hand, loving me, and taking care of me will never happen. Even though she tells me she loves me all the time, I feel nothing when I hear it. I won the "feeling nothing" lottery. Nothing but emptiness from that woman.

Therein lies so much of the battle in my head. As a child, I needed, wanted, and craved the love and attention my parents should have given me. As an adult, I have completely outgrown my parents. They are narrow-minded, hypocritical, negative people. Still, they have seeped into my vulgar, gullible, vulnerable, somewhat diabolical behavior. Oh, how wide my pendulum swings. On one side, I want and crave love, and, on the other side, I think "you're too stupid and narrow-minded for my time." Angry much? I still run to the negative, even when I'm feeling positive. I have those amazing bursts of energy—a moment of solace where everything seems to be flowing smoothly, and, suddenly, the brain goes insane.

Even though my pendulum swings are caused by an unstable relationship with my mother, I don't consistently tell my children I love them. The words simply don't leave my lips easily.

After all, they're just words, right? I read somewhere that "love" is a verb, and therefore requires doing. I do, every day, for my children—I just don't tell them. I just do it. Should I tell them more? Will it help them when they get older? "Hey, I was at your game," . . . "Look at the lunch I packed for you today, all with love," . . . "Gee, dear, let me help you with your homework" . . . NOPE! I don't do it verbally, I just do it. Take that, Nike. I'm raising astute kids. They know how much I love them, and they know I'm here. They can "feel" it. They don't need to "hear" it all day. In my head, love is about sacrifice. Simply doing the things I want to do when I want to do them is not always possible. Giving of yourself for the betterment of another. That's my kids. I give a lot of myself, and they KNOW I love them, and I am there for them always.

Sometimes I think I have the answers to all of these questions, but sometimes I think I'm just as lost as always. Inner peace and "calm," where do they come from? I'm in my forties, and it's time for me to figure it out. I don't want to live another forty years with all of this inner turmoil. I do yoga, but still my busy brain is thinking about everything else I have to do while in a downward dog position. Crap. That's actually usually when I'm thinking about sex. The instructor is constantly telling us to "stay in the room," mind and body. My body is there, but my mind isn't. I've been to a spiritual healer. I've had my numerology done. I've had my astrology done. I've even been to an energy healer. Some of the information was so dead on, but some of it was completely off. I refuse to believe my neck pain is caused from being a beheaded monk in my past life—although that might explain my high testosterone levels.

I've tried all these solutions, but nothing will completely train my mind. You can't take the lion out of a lion. I don't know if I'll ever be that quiet, zen-ful being. But I have come to a place where I am a more "mindful" person. I'm a work in progress, but at least I'm "in progress." I still harbor anger and resentment for my parents, but to a much lesser degree. I'm still pissed about all the pedophiles out there still harming children. That anger and passion simply won't go away, and that's good because I know addressing the issue is my calling. I'll forever be a survivor of sexual abuse, and I won't stop with my mission to end it. Or, at the very least, get people talking about it, even if it makes them uncomfortable.

How I handle my emotions is my responsibility, and it took a virus-induced mess of a car accident to realize it. For example, I am taking control of my anger and passion. Are they the same thing? In certain conversations, I believe they are. I know I have the wherewithal and intellect to control *how* I direct my anger and passion. Sometimes, however, my mouth erupts, too—much like the insane diarrhea I had. More often than not, I can't be perfect, and that's fine with me. You know how much I love the word "perfect."

The universe is far from perfect, and the same is true about people, as well. We are sloppy, imperfect beings who make mistakes. That's how we learn. Now that's powerful. Learn and grow, much like my kids. Do we ever stop growing? Stopping should be one of the deadly sins. We are taught to not be gluttonous, lustful, slothful, greedy, prideful, envious, or full of wrath. Now, I am adding one more—don't be stagnant. We should always want to grow, whether as children or adults, and especially as empathetic humans.

While I am done being this floating and lost soul, it is a never-ending quest of self-discovery. I don't want the negative self-talk there anymore. I am searching for something, and, with my personality, I will find it. I will be kicking, screaming, and scratching until I find "calm." They say you have to go through the eye of the storm to find the calm waters. Well, I am in the eye of the storm, and it's rocky as hell, but I'll find those calm waters.

Until then, and, while on my journey, I have no other choice but to be the strong, compassionate, loving woman for my children. The loving one, and, sadly, at times, the lost one. Sometimes, I feel like I'm just fooling everyone but myself. If only I had learned properly, maybe I wouldn't need to play this game. I don't want my children to ever feel the way I feel. I want them to feel at peace, to be able to sit quietly, to be able to sleep, and to close down their minds, knowing they are loved. I don't ever want their minds racing like mine always does—I want my children to know peace.

All of these realizations stemmed from one morning of illness that showed me how lucky I am to be alive. Aren't we all lucky to be alive? I don't want you to experience illness and a bad car accident to come to this realization. You're much luckier than you think you are, especially if you're sharing this moment with me. It means we've come together through something bigger than ourselves. I love to hang on to that thought.

Chapter 21

Changing Mindsets One Honest Word at a Time

"There's not enough tape to keep this mouth closed."

—"Wild Hearts Can't Be Broken," Pink—

I've talked about my past. I've talked about how I'm trying to move on. I've talked about the long-term effects of adverse childhood experiences. I've talked about the sexual abuse I endured. I've defined pedophilia. I've talked about a lot of uncomfortable subjects in this book. The '70s are over. I will never be assaulted again by any pedophile. It's no longer about me; it's about what's happening right now, whether it's in your home or your neighbor's. It's happening whether you like it or not. It's time to talk about right now. I've realized that my purpose is combating and stopping the perverts and pedophiles who so tragically alter their victims' lives. When I set out on advancing this cause, I knew creating change would not be easy. The taboo subject of child sexual abuse has been ignored for decades, if not centuries. I had embarked on one hell of an undertaking: to get people to change their inherent, lifelong way of thinking, but it *needs* to be changed.

I kept asking myself what I could do to start changing the way people think about sexual abuse, and, ultimately, act upon this information. Awareness is obviously not enough. April is Child Abuse Awareness Month, but there are another eleven months in each year where this is still a huge problem. This is a twenty-four-hour-a-day, seven-day-a-week problem. Couldn't they have at least chosen a month with thirty-one days? I guess I should be thankful they didn't choose February. My mission is to start changing the way people see child sexual abuse, from an abstract issue to a real possibility. The bottom line is it's easy to talk about strangers. It's damn near impossible to look at your child and ask, "Is your father or stepfather touching you inappropriately?" We all engage in those heart-wrenching, horrific conversations about child sex trafficking and child abduction, and it's innate for mothers to protect their children from strangers. Even my own mother was aghast when nine-year-old Amber Hagerman was abducted and murdered in 1996, just thirty miles from my mother's home in Texas. Of course, the AMBER alert, which is also an acronym for "America's Missing Broadcast Emergency Response," is named after this child victim. I remember watching her respond to this news and her comment, "I can't believe there are monsters out there like this. That poor, sweet girl." Never mind the monster she slept next to every night that she chose to ignore. What if she had been educated to understand and talk about sexual assault differently?

I wanted to take action in my own life, so I decided to start locally. I called a friend of mine, a teacher at my son's elementary school. She was adored by all and was a damn good teacher. I wanted to see what she could do to start the conversation with young kids at the prime age for being targets of sexual abuse. Unfortunately, she responded that it made her sick to her stomach to even *think* that any one of her students could currently be experiencing sexual abuse. Of course! It should make us sick to the core! Simply put, she said she was scared to lose her job if she said anything about sexual abuse in the classroom. The topic would raise eyebrows and upset the parents. It would cause an uproar in the community. I did understand her position. It's not like she could have said, "OKAY, for a treat today, we're having chocolate muffins, and, by the way, was anyone touched inappropriately last night?" I get it! So—what should we do? Where do we go? How do we protect them?

Let's do some simple math here. There are nearly six-hundred children in this elementary school, and we'll assume about half are girls. One in four girls will be sexually abused by the time they turn eighteen. That's seventy-five girls out of the six-hundred kids in our school. There are twenty-five classes, so that would be three little girls in each class, and I'm not even accounting for the little boys in the school. These are just numbers. Sheer numbers. Statistics. Everyone has to take statistics in college. We should all understand how they work, right?

Our school has been ranked one of the top elementary schools in the state of Texas. We live in what they call, "the bubble." We are in the heart of a prominent, good Christian community. Surely, these statistics don't apply to us. Check again. Sexual abuse knows no socio-economic boundaries. Do you remember when I wrote that my mother and step-pedophlia father were excellent Christians, too? It's difficult to trust any religion, race, or creed to save our kids from being abused. Unfortunately, it's all too common across every divide. Why are we so afraid to talk about "it?" Why can't we "open the dialogue," and keep it open? Listen, I'm not a certified teacher. I don't know how to talk to children in a group setting, but I have made the boundaries between acceptable and unacceptable *very clear* to my children from day one.

I know that, to make an impact, I need the freedom to talk about this very real issue without the stigma. Who doesn't want freedom? Freedom with a safety net? Sure. Freedom with boundaries? We all need those. We crave them. We can't live without them. Boundaries make us feel safe. For me, breaking boundaries means more because of my past. When you're abused, you're being held down, forced to do things you don't want to do, and you're being completely controlled. For two long years, I had to do things that made me feel horrible, dirty, ashamed, and terrified. As I grew up, I realized the trust around me was broken, and I hated the control that stole my purity and innocence.

Now, I like pushing boundaries. I go to the edge. I look over, and I wonder, *what if?* What if I jump? Will something catch me before I hit the bottom? I want the exhilaration, but not at the risk of losing my life. Luckily, I've always had a safety net to catch me, like my ex-husband. He caught me through many a fall, and I suppose he still does. My impulsivity is still there, but not nearly as often or as reckless, as it used to be. When it is there, I have a lifeline: I have Richard to help keep me grounded. Like the time a mother tried to aggressively intervene in my parenting, so I told her she needed to do herself a favor, get laid, and calm her nerves. I just *had to* open my mouth and intervene. We understand my mouth by now, right? My no-filter, take-no-prisoners mouth. She threatened to call the police (great, but I don't think they are in the business of fucking lonely housewives), but Richard was there to mediate. Another disaster averted. Richard is my lifeline and my safety net.

I have serious control issues, and with, control issues, come inevitable trust issues. Even simple things like getting on a plane causes me anxiety. Is the pilot competent? Did he drink last night? Can he land this bird? Are we going to crash? Does that sound paranoid? My defense mechanisms apply to almost all people and all situations. Even *the person flying the plane* needs to earn my trust. Really, Wanda? Put Amy to bed. In these cases, I try to remind myself to use my wise mind, rather than my emotional one. I'm sure the entire aviation industry has confirmed that the pilot is more than qualified. But then again, they're controlling everything and I'm not. Control is the safety net I have built for myself. The more I recognize this, the more I realize I need to work on it.

I'm working on being less impulsive, but I still find it hard to control the one thing I physically can: my mouth. I want freedom of speech. I need to feel safe. I need boundaries. But how do we *ever* feel free to express what we're feeling without a safety net? I've always been aggressive, and I've always been tough, both mentally and physically. Was I born this way, or did these suck-ass experiences make me the person I am today? As an adult mother of four beautiful, incredible children, I'm realizing I need to temper my instincts a bit. A "bit," though, is the key word. I believe my voice needs to be heard, because this is such an important subject. I have important things to say—and I say them in a way people want to hear. I'm *funny*. But let's face it, many of the things I say are still hard to stomach. If I can use this "gift" to raise awareness and educate people about a topic that is so very important, yet so very taboo, hopefully people see the value in taking the good with the bad. If I wasn't so blunt and outspoken, I wouldn't be able to do what I feel I'm called to do.

Writing has been one of the keys to my healing. I've had to dig deep to try and answer questions that may never have an answer. Maybe some questions aren't *meant* to have answers, but my resilience is strong, and so is my ability to be numb, which is something I don't want. Maybe I feel too much. Here's what I know as a fact: I would never allow anyone to molest my child, or *any* child for that matter. I would never walk away from my children or make them feel unimportant. They are the most important part of my life. I will give my children what they want and need—within reason, of course. I've always been eager and ready to do fun things. I believe in a home built on safety and security. How ironic that I've made a career as a homebuilder! Each time I complete a project, I hope they will have a wonderful life with the families that live there.

After I published one of my blogs and shared it with my friends on Facebook, a friend of mine posted a comment. "Way to go, Wanda. You're changing the world one honest word at a time. Thank you." Wow. That's affirmation. Many people have private messaged me, telling me their horrific story of abuse. A friend of mine asked me at what point did I start to enjoy sex? She had major issues with intimacy after her brother molested her. Yep. *Her brother*—for years. I'm happy my friend was able to share her story with me, even if it's thirty or forty years after the fact. It feels good to unleash. I'm not sure how many other people who have reached out to me in a private manner have told anyone else about their abuse. The biting honesty of my blog has allowed others to contact me and share their stories. Perhaps I'm onto something here. The hardest part for any of us is to reach out and tell someone about our experience, isn't it? Don't be afraid. Talk to me, or someone you feel you can trust. Don't be afraid of being judged.

After being a guest on *One Life Radio* last year, they asked me to come back a few months later. I guess my mouth didn't scare them too badly. I'd been on the show solo, but next time they wanted me to come on with a psychologist. They wanted me to discuss how being sexually abused as a child affects your relationships as an adult. My only comment to the producer was, "We only have an hour?" That's because I have a lot to say to anyone who's personally connected to my story, either as a victim or as a pervert. The most important thing I say to victims—on my blog, in radio shows, and in any other venue that will have me—is *you've done nothing wrong.* Let me be very clear about that. When I told my mother my story and she blamed me, it put me through years of shameful hell.

In order to help others, I had to take the steps to help myself and distance myself from those years of hell. I had to take stock in my strengths to build confidence in myself, which brings me to my favorite sport: hockey. I love those moments in life when someone says to me, "You play hockey, seriously?" Usually followed by a strange look, and then a second glance. "Really!!! I do," I reassure them. I'm sure that disbelief comes from the fact that I have all of my teeth. They are all in their original position, and my face is completely intact. For me, sports are a reflection of life. I'd rather be in the game versus sitting on the bench. I've never been much of a spectator. As much as I enjoyed being a volunteer coach with the YMCA, I still have this deep-rooted passion to play, even with fifty knocking on my door. I want to be out there playing, growing, evolving, and living. Brene Brown asks, in her book, *Daring Greatly*, "Wouldn't you rather be in the ring, fighting the fight, versus sitting in the cheap seats, judging and staring?" Experience life. Try new things! Bring it! I think you've gleaned thus far that I'm not your "traditional" type of girl. I like to challenge myself and those around me, probably because it's harder to hit a moving target. I have this deep need to keep moving, to challenge myself, to challenge my relationships with men, and to push my kids a bit harder. Sports, my true love, fills my need for constant stimulation. I may be a bit slower today, but I still play.

When I was thirty, I took advantage of the opportunity to play tackle football in a women's league. It was surreal. Finally, I could play. Girls didn't play tackle football in Texas, in the '80s and '90s. Are you kidding me? Title IX, my ass. I was always picked last when playing with the boys down the street, but I showed them. I can do anything. "You throw like a girl." Damn right. And it's further than you throw, you smug little shit. I finally donned the pads at thirty years old. Real pads. Real tackle football. Real. Real. Real. The experience was surreal. I suited up as both the kicker and the punter. All 5'2" of me can easily kick a forty-yard field goal. Last time I tried, I easily kicked a thirty-yarder, but that's when I was eight months pregnant with my fourth child. Kicker was the perfect position for me: I understand exactly why there's a "roughing the kicker" penalty (stick with me on this one). The offensive line (my mother) was supposed to protect the kicker (me, a sitting duck) from the defensive line (the pedophile). Sadly, I had a small line who was unable to stop the defense from penetrating (bad pun) the offensive line and BAM—they took me out! Flags flying everywhere. Whistles blown. The ref calls the penalty. I suppose being the kicker in football is very metaphorical for me. Where was my referee to give the pedophile his penalty? If only my parents had done their job, I wouldn't have been hurt so badly.

Football reminds me of the hits I've taken, but hockey shows me the hits I can keep on giving. I started playing hockey at thirty-three, after the birth of my third child.

And I wasn't just turning thirty-three—I was raising three kids on top of teaching myself how to play hockey. I couldn't have been more inept at skating, puck handling, or even understanding the rules of the game, but I tried. I tried and failed, and tried and failed again, but that's just me. I'm Wanda, and I can do anything! Right? Wrong . . . Okay . . . I really sucked at it. I could do anything with a soccer ball, but I could not skate. Plus, it was a foreign sport in Dallas: we only had one small skating rink at the mall that I went to once a year during the holidays, to test my skills at skating. Everything about this felt unnatural. Teaching myself to do something I'd never done at this age was no easy task, especially at 5'2" when some of these women are the size of NFL linemen. They chase after you with a look in their eyes, like they want to tear you apart.

Now, though, I've headed to Tampa every year since I turned forty, for USA Hockey's national tournament. It's another testament to the fact that I can do anything I set my mind to. This year, I will head to Tampa with two of my brood (it's always easier with two instead of four) and my teammates to defend our National Championship from the prior year. I beam with pride when I see my name hanging high on that banner at my ice rink. The very same rink where I had to figure out how to stop without a brake. Why would I care about some banner at a smelly ice rink? It represents the choices I made to challenge myself and live my life and NOT sit on the sidelines. I have an actual banner that says, "National Champions." Not bad for a girl growing up in that fucked-up household. I'm successful despite my parents, not because of them. Who knows, maybe your name will be on a banner hanging high in the sky. How awesome would that be?

I'm competitive, and I do like to win—with an asterisk. Let me be very clear about this: I only like to win when the competition is evenly matched. Ever been on the end of an ass whipping? Ever given one? Whether I'm playing, coaching, or watching as a parent on the sideline, it's never fun for me if it's an uneven match. I try to deemphasize winning as a top priority when I coach. We, as a society, are so focused on winning, but, if you ask me about my win-loss record, I honestly have no clue.

For ten years, I volunteered as a volleyball coach at the YMCA. I gave hundreds of hours of my time, if not more. My biggest win is that I've had the same core group of girls for eight seasons. Most of these girls had never even touched a volleyball before the third grade. These tiny little eight-year-old girls had so much innocence in their eyes. I remember my life at that age—that was when my sexual abuse began. I knew in my heart that I could make a difference in their lives. They certainly weren't the most athletic girls, but they had heart. You can teach skill, but you can't teach heart. After many seasons of hard work, we finally won the championship. We were down significantly in the last game, and I had given up hope, but they hadn't. They came back and went on to win. I was *stunned* by the sheer tenacity of these girls that sent them soaring past their opponent. I remember the elation these girls felt; no one can ever take that away from them. It's youth sports at its best moment. I had three rules as a coach. My first rule as a coach was to always have fun. I couldn't remember my other two, so I reached out to my daughter while writing this book, to ask her what the other two were. Her response was, "All I remember is have fun." I guess I hit the mark I was intending.

I also coached my older daughter's team, but we never won a championship. That didn't matter. We won a different sort of championship because we had a player with Down's Syndrome. I questioned my ability to effectively coach her, but I soon realized that putting a check in the win column wasn't that important. Just her sending the ball over the net was a win. The girls would pile on top of her when she got a serve over the net. *That was a win in my book!* The compassion these girls felt for her simply amazed me. The team was there for her, and they were there for each other, whether we won or lost.

Clearly, there are other factors we must measure besides the score. Wins and losses only tell part of the story. When little boys are booing, is that a win? No, it's definitely a loss. When parents berate anyone and act like spoiled, impetuous children, is that a win? Um, no. It's a loss. When a child finally gets that free throw in for the first time or finally makes contact with the ball from the bat? Is that a win? Most definitely. My point in all this is that the final score is not the only indicator of a successful game. It only tells part of the story, but, sadly, that's what we measure most, as it's so objective. Everything else is subjective. Now, if your kid is vying to become the next Dallas Cowboy or Los Angeles Laker, then GO FOR IT. I get that. But when your kid is on the field and giving his or her all, then shut the fuck up and let that kid feel supported. Cause I'm telling you, as a mother, an athlete, and a coach, it pays off in the end. Instead of counting wins versus losses, why don't we count good behavior versus bad behavior, good character versus bad character, and good choices versus bad choices? Maybe those things are far better indicators to gauge the success of youth sports than the win/loss ticker.

Writing. Talking. Coaching. Playing. These are all the steps I have taken to confront the effects of my path, but I know now the wounds will never be fully healed. It's less like a scar and more like a complete overhaul of my nervous system. To this day, I'm still not 100% comfortable in my own home, which is not a good thing, when I have children and dogs to care for. I sleep with my door closed. It's not like a dead molester will come into my bedroom, but my brain hasn't quite processed that fact, and the fear remains. My heart rate still goes up when I'm alone in my bed at night, and I berate myself for it. I realize I am being ridiculous. After all, my abuser is dead, and I am a grown woman, but I still feel afraid. I want to feel safe in my own home. It was a challenge to figure out how to give my children a safe and loving home when my own mother had not modeled that for me. I'm successful, a good mother, I have amazing friends, and I'm proud that I'm a determined woman that gets things done. Perhaps I'm not as numb as before, but there is a twinge there, a fear that can't be denied. I know I'm no longer harboring a secret, but I still numb myself and *that* makes me even angrier. I know I am not alone in this fear. Many people feel this way, too. Someone told me once, "If you feel it, it's real. If they feel it, it's real." There's a lot of talk about PTSD these days, which is very real for me and why I still close my bedroom door at night.

I finally understand what happened to me has had long-term detrimental effects. Knowing there are people out there still hurting children is a daily trigger for me. The subject can't be avoided—it's in the news almost constantly, yet very few have the kinds of conversations I'm trying to encourage. I talk about these insecurities in hopes that I might help encourage anyone feeling the same way to speak up. I started the "One Blunt Woman" podcast because I'm pretty sure there's no other podcast out there where you can find a weekly pedophile report. *Call me.* Talk to me. Or talk to a shrink, a counselor, or someone you trust. From the minister, to the coach, to the stepfather, to the boyfriend, to the babysitter—no one is off limits.

I've come out and shared my story in spite of my mother's early discouragement and am talking about this subject because I want you to feel safe and open up, too. If you don't know anyone you can trust, you can always call the National Sexual Assault Hotline at 1-800-656-HOPE (4673). They are available to speak with you twenty-four hours a day, seven days a week. The RAAIN Organization (Rape, Abuse, and Incest National Network) is the nation's largest anti-sexual violence organization, and they have trained staff members who can provide you with confidential crisis support online or over the phone. The most valuable thing they have is the capability to protect your privacy. But no matter what, *please* talk to someone. I remember when I didn't feel like I could talk to anyone about my abuse, as you've read in my previous chapters. The quote, "That which does not get resolved remains," definitely applies here. "Preservatives," whether they were internal or external, were keeping my secret alive and extending the shelf life of my secret. I don't want anyone to suffer in silence. It's not necessary, especially when there is so much help available to you.

Time is the only way I can ever truly trust someone. With all the pedophiles out there in our everyday lives, I doubt I'll ever be a person who trusts easily, but I know that talking helps. Getting the ghosts out of the closet, out of our bedrooms, and out of our *hearts* may just give us the safety nets we're searching for, as well as the boundaries we need to feel safer.

Writing this book, doing my podcast, playing and coaching sports, and excelling in raising my children have brought me some form of comfort and joy. Learning to thrive in an environment so foreign to me, where I am uncomfortable, would become one of my top priorities. Writing this book and talking about my past has made me realize my intrinsic need to help victims of sexual abuse. I would find a much-needed release in sports and achievements, but, truly, it is my need to be fearless that has sustained me throughout my life. Parts of me can see the light at the end of the proverbial tunnel (aka peace), but I still have some angry tracks ahead of me that need to be removed.

Is anything holding you back? Are you making excuses? We all have plenty. I say, "Lace up and get your ass on the ice!" Go wherever you want to go and do whatever you want to do in order to be happy. I like it when people are happy and content. You will be challenged, and, at times, you will fall. Yes, it will hurt, and, sometimes, it will hurt a lot more than you want it to. Or, you could just sit on the sidelines and watch. It's a choice that's all yours, not mine. I'm just trying to figure out what my next crazy adventure will be. Maybe you'll choose something like being a really good mom to your kids. I admire that. Though I would much rather you got on the ice with me. We'll be gentle.

NOT. Get out there. Take a chance on something. I know you can do it.

Chapter 22

Forgiveness in Your Forties Is Possible

"I may be old and I may be young,
but I am not done changing."

—"Changing," John Mayer—

I f you want something in life, you really gotta sink your teeth into it. OKAY. Bad pun. But that is what I learned at the age of eight. Those were the choices I was given. Can you even, for one moment, fathom someone coming to you or your eight-year-old daughter and making that request?

It happens every single day. Still to this day. It will shape so many others' experiences, just like it has shaped mine, for many years to come.

Writing this is so fucking dismal. Even I am disgusted. There is no romanticizing this part of history. Look what I learned at such a young age. Horrific. I learned how to become a survivor. It did turn me into an athlete because it was my escape mechanism, but I wish I could have honed my athletic talents the normal way. You know, the one where the parent comes outside and throws the ball to you, and you get to throw it back. They smile and say, "Good girl, great job," not, "Oh that feels good." You may think I'm making light of the situation, but thank God I'm in my mid-forties, now, and can laugh at this. All great comedians come out of a childhood full of tragedy; I am no exception. Not that I am a great comedian, but I can be funny at times and certainly twisted. I made this choice about my personality. It gives me relief from so much of the resentment and anger that has built up over the years. Laughing is such a reprieve from being held down emotionally. I have something to say, and, by God, I will say it.

I've also tried to learn more about what was psychologically happening to me because of the sexual abuse I endured. I've questioned, for example, why I said "yes" to getting that backpack, despite what I had to do to get it. Why didn't I walk away? I finally realized he was going to do what he regularly did, anyway. If the game that time was for me to get a backpack, then so be it. It's not like he was going to stop. I instinctively knew then and now. I also question how developed could my brain have been at eight years old. I've learned how the brain of an eight-year-old girl develops *normally*. At this stage, children typically:

- Develop critical and abstract thinking skills.

- Develop their own games with complicated rules.

- Become skilled in reading, writing, and use of oral language.

- Begin to express creative skills through writing, acting, inventing, and designing.

- Ask many questions to develop their own point of view.

- Begin to collect things and develop an interest in projects.

- Care about fairness; develop a sense of right and wrong.

- Develop competitiveness.

- Start to understand puns and riddles.

- Become curious as to how things work and how they are made.

To me, this makes a lot of sense. Much of this applied to me, especially with "inventing, designing, competitiveness, and curiosity." I had to build my own Barbie house. Today, they call it Mind Craft, but, back then, I had to use books and my own imagination, and it turned out beautifully. Today, I live in a house that I built. I was hands-on in every aspect of having the house I desired and loved so much. Yet, despite building such a great house, I find it challenging to build a great home. Home is where the heart is, truly, but it's impossible to go unscathed when you're abused as a child; however, it has been proven that if the perpetrator is removed from the home where the abuse occurred, the child has a far greater chance of a healthy life as an adult. When a child is believed and rescued, she is given hope, which is way more than I was ever given. It's not always possible to stop the abuse before it happens, but the moment the abuse is revealed and the parent finds out, it's time for them to step in and make damn sure it doesn't happen again. I can't blame my mother for not stopping the abuse when it happened, as she didn't know at that time. I blame the pedophile. But fuck, where was she when I finally got the courage to tell her? She had one simple choice to make, and she couldn't do it. Some may say, "Wanda, get over your childhood. It's over." People tell me that all the time, and I fully agree with that statement. I just wish it was only the sexual abuse that I had to "get over." I don't know if I'll ever "get over it," but I'm sure as hell not going to repeat it or sit idly by and watch it happen to someone else. I have turned my anger into passion so that I can use my passion to make a difference for others.

Choices are something we all have to make each and every day. I learned at a **VERY** young age how to make choices, and, now, I've made the wisest choice of them all. I'm going to talk about my life, the bad decisions I've made, the hurt I feel inside, and the reasons behind it all. Then, I'm going to make a choice to stand up for children everywhere, so we can unite and be a voice for those who feel they don't have one.

After that, we're all going to Disneyland. Or the beach.

I make some good and bad choices when it comes to parenting. Hell, every parent does. Luckily, my girls have never experienced this atrocity, and, with any luck, never will. I've made it a point to tell my girls to never let a person touch them. Ever. If a man ever touched my girls or my boys, I would cut off his dick and feed it to him in pieces. These monsters (take out the "n" and add in "le," and you go from monster to molester) should have all their human rights stripped from them. All of them. Feed them to the lions! Let's see who has the control then!

There are girls and women out there faced with sexual and emotional abuse every day. It's numbing to think they have no choice, but they do. They can tell someone. Anyone. A mother, sister, aunt, friend, teacher, or anyone they trust. I just hope that person believes them and it doesn't backfire. I can never really figure out why my mother would let that man sit across the table from me, knowing what he had done to me. What the fuck is wrong with her? What is wrong with any woman who lets a man touch her daughter and does nothing? What am I missing? I feel I am still full of anger, hate, and resentment—and even still, from time to time, shame rears its ugly head.

I cannot sit back and allow this to be a silent crime. It infuriates me to no end that people won't talk about this, or they sweep it under the rug. I'm going to make so much noise about this that millions will stand up with me to help conquer the sexual abuse of children. We're going to talk about this epidemic of "hush, hush" and "don't talk about it," and about how we're opening our eyes and lifting our voices to help millions of girls, so they may have a chance at a normal life. I'm mean, *come on!* Let's teach our girls at a young age to protect themselves.

There are breast cancer walks, heart walks, and now we're going to create a "Walk to End Sexual Abuse" or, better yet, a "Keep Your Dick in the Box" (my take on Justin Timberlake's SNL skit) walk or "Survivors of Hell" walk. We'll figure out an appropriate name together, but I love the idea of a safe haven for women and men to join together, talk, walk, and hopefully laugh and learn that the abuse isn't going to define them. We are *not* the ones in the wrong, and it's *not* our fault. Our voices will be heard in unison with millions coming together, and, if we can stop one child from being abused, we've done our job and have made a significant impact on some lives. I know we can help. Sexual abuse cannot be a silent subject any longer because being molested is not a choice any child makes. If abuse can be avoided, that child's life can be granted so many more positive outcomes.

Thank you for taking this journey with me. It's been a crazy one. I hope this book does something different for you than those usual words of encouragement. You know the ones: "How can you love someone else, if you don't love yourself? It takes a strong person to say sorry and a stronger one to forgive. Forgiveness is a gift you give yourself." I could go on for days. I believe in a few of these phrases, and also think some of them are a bunch of shit. Aren't we all a work in progress? Isn't it the hard times that make us stronger? "That which does not break you, makes you stronger." It's really more like, "What doesn't kill you, gives you a set of unhealthy coping mechanisms and a dark sense of humor." So why do I feel broken so much of the time? Why does it take every ounce of strength some days to pull myself together? Why are some things instant triggers for me?

You know my story now. The ordeal is real. It stays with you for a lifetime, and the insecurities may stay with you for what feels like many lifetimes. Do I forgive the molester? Do I forgive my mother? Do I forgive my absentee father? Do I forgive myself? And what is the order? How does that work? There are so many books and movies that have the same meaning when it comes to forgiveness. Especially the old adage, "I did the best I could with what I knew at the time." That statement definitely pertains to my mother. I've forgiven my mother for being weak. Maybe it was the times and the era in which she grew up, or maybe it was just part of her DNA. I don't know. I asked her in therapy recently, and she stated she doesn't remember much of what I told her when I was twelve. Perhaps it's the early stages of Alzheimer's that has set in. Who really knows at this point? More than likely I will never get "closure" (oh, there's that word) for our relationship. So, therein lies my conundrum. Do I forgive her anyway, so my heart can heal? Will it heal? It's worth trying, I suppose.

I've worked hard on forgiving the molester, which is still a work in progress because so much of who I am today is because of what he did to me. He's dead, so it's inconsequential to me at this point, but I did do my job as a mother by never letting him around my daughters. And then there is my dad. Oh boy! I don't know how I feel about him; I have so many tumultuous feelings. If only he had been there for me, perhaps so much of my fucked-up-ness wouldn't be so present in my life today. I'm working harder on healing than anything else. It's true what they say; emotional scars stay with you long after physical ones disappear. And there it is, folks. So many bad decisions made by the most influential people in my life have brought me here today.

How does one deal with all of these issues and not the backlash that goes with it? How do we get through the eye of the storm and hope to come out alive? I know I'm a strong woman. I have that. I also have four amazing human beings that count on me day in and day out. I count on them, too. They validate me, and that is an amazing feeling. Not just because I am their mother, but because I give them what they need, for the most part. At least the damage my parents and stepparents have caused me hasn't damaged my ability to love my own children.

Maybe I can start with that, and grow from there. It all boils down to forgiveness, which is something I haven't 100% arrived at. I'm aiming for forgiveness, but I'm not there yet. Forgiveness is a work in progress, and I would love to hear your thoughts on the subject. I think banding together and making a difference in someone else's world does help heal old wounds. Perhaps that's what forgiveness is in the end. Simply being a good person, knowing your worth, doing right by others, and, when someone needs you, being there for them. Above all, love yourself and be good to you.

My good friend cracked me up when she said, "Control is an illusion. Eventually you will learn the only thing you want to or hope to control is your bladder." Maybe peace will come with menopause, along with new-found hair on my face. The Lord giveth and the Lord taketh away. "Lord help me, I'm not ending this book with the Lord."

Maybe there is hope, after all, for faith in God. I know that no one will be shoving anything down my throat, literally or figuratively, without my approval, unless they want to lose their anatomical parts. Therefore, even my belief systems are my own and not swayed by anyone who "thinks" they're doing well by and/or for me. I can make my own decisions, and most of them are actually pretty good.

There isn't much I can do to get answers at this point, anyway, so it's on me. One thing I can do is work my ass off to stop as many pedophiles as I can in this lifetime. *That* would heal my heart. I want to save the children of the world. Yes, you read that right. I want to save the children. I don't want them touched or harmed in any way. I can't do it by myself. I need your help. So many people turn a blind eye to what is going on, but I can only hope that changes. With our access to social media, and, with people finally stepping up and owning their behavior, change is on the horizon.

It's not The End. It's The Beginning. I hope you're uncomfortable enough to be the change we wish to see in the world. I hope this book resonates with you, and that all of the hell I've been through will push you to help yourself and help a child. Don't be blind to what is going on. Be proactive. It all comes down to the choices we make—and the lives we can save from potential abusers.

This Section's All Yours
What's Your Role Moving Forward?

1. What activities help you calm your mind or get out your anger? If you don't have one, take some time to punch a pillow, scream a bit, then signup for some intermural football.

2. What gives you comfort and joy?

3. In what ways are you working on forgiveness?

4. How do you give back to your community? How have you been able to nurture your roots?

5. Is there any one you can think of who might benefit from this book? How will you share this story?

6. What action can you take to stop the perverts out there? Or, what steps can you take to start the conversation about child molestation in your area?

About the Author

Wanda Means is One Blunt Woman. After surviving childhood sexual abuse by her stepfather and coping with the subsequent abandonment, rejection, and neglect, Wanda is ready to be brutally honest. In her blog and in her podcast titled "One Blunt Woman," Wanda is the first to admit she has a big mouth—and she plans to use it. Her blogging, podcasting, and writing revolve around having real conversations, ranging from abuse and pedophilia, to parenting, to sex and relationships, to finding her feet in the world of online dating. Most importantly, though, she's sending out harsh words and a tough message to abusers out there.

Wanda's no-bullshit, can-do attitude is rounded out by her work and home life. She is a successful real estate developer and a single mother of four. She is also an avid hockey player and has won the USA Hockey's "Over Forty" National Championship. She was born in Dallas, Texas, where she still lives with her children.

CPSIA information can be obtained
at www.ICGtesting.com
Printed in the USA
BVHW06s0926020518
515050BV00018B/495/P